# MEMORIAL:
# THE MYSTERY OF
# MARY OF BETHANY

Dolores Kimball

Ɛ P

**EP BOOKS**

Faverdale North

Darlington

DL3 0PH, England


web: http://www.epbooks.org


e-mail: sales@epbooks.org


EP Books are distributed in the USA by:

JPL Distribution

3741 Linden Avenue Southeast

Grand Rapids, MI 49548

E-mail: orders@jpldistribution.com

Tel: 877.683.6935

First published 2014


British Library Cataloguing in Publication Data available


ISBN 978-0-85234-963-2

All Scripture quotes are from the New King James Version, unless otherwise noted.

# Contents

# Introduction

I've always been fascinated by the story of Mary of
Bethany. For years I've pondered the words of Jesus
spoken as Mary anointed him for his burial: 'Assuredly,
I say to you, wherever this gospel is preached in the
whole world, what this woman has done will also be told
as a memorial to her' (Matthew 26:13; Mark 14:9). What
on earth, I've always wondered, could she possibly have
done to merit such an extraordinary commendation
from the Lord? The more I looked into it, and the more
I learned of Mary, the more I came to believe that hers
is an honest-to-goodness, read-between-the-lines mystery
story, a mystery that revolves around Jesus' tribute to her,
a tribute unique in all of Scripture.

If we dig deep enough, we can uncover the portrait of
a fascinating woman. It's all there, but it takes looking
not merely at what she said and did, but also at what her
words, and especially her actions, revealed about her
heart. We've all heard the story of Mary and Martha.
Perhaps too many times. Why, then, is Mary's story a

mystery? In spite of all the books written and sermons preached about the two sisters, Mary of Bethany is not often seen for who she is—one of the most amazing, unique, and inspirational women in all of Scripture.

For one thing, Mary is one of only four individuals in the Bible whom Jesus personally commended. In that regard, she ranks right up there with John the Baptist, about whom Jesus said there was no greater man born of woman (Luke 7:28), and the Roman centurion whose faith, Jesus said, was greater than all those in Israel (Matthew 8:5–10). Mary of Bethany also takes her place beside one other woman in receiving Jesus' commendation, the Canaanite woman whose great faith Jesus lauded (Matthew 15:22–28).

But not even these three received a tribute comparable to that given to Mary. For her act alone did Jesus offer this high praise. For what exactly was Jesus praising Mary? Why did her actions—in this case anointing his head with oil for his burial—cause Jesus to honor her? What was the good work Mary performed? What did she know about Jesus' death that the disciples couldn't, or wouldn't, understand? Perhaps most mysterious is why Scripture records so little of the words of Mary. How could a woman who said so little be worthy of such accolades from the Lord? These and other questions about the character of Mary of Bethany will be answered in the following chapters, and by solving the mystery of Mary, we will see life-changing truths women today will find inspiring and encouraging. First, though, we must start by answering the question of who Mary of Bethany was, and equally important, who she was not.

In researching this book, I found another mystery. How can it be that the woman whose sacred act of worship Jesus said would be told down through the ages and throughout the world is frequently mistaken for a prostitute, the sinful woman in Luke 7 who also anointed Jesus' feet? This is not only untrue; it does a tremendous disservice to Mary. She is also confused with Mary Magdalene, who is herself confused with the sinful woman. Mary was from the small town of Bethany, located on the Eastern slope of the Mount of Olives, about two miles from Jerusalem. She was the sister of Martha, and had a brother named Lazarus, whom Jesus raised from the dead. Mary Magdalene was from the area of northern Palestine called Magdala, and there is no reference to anyone of her family. Mary Magdalene is nowhere identified as a prostitute or as a sinful woman, despite popular portrayals of her as such. The only thing we know about her past is that Jesus cast seven demons out of her (Mark 16:9; Luke 8:2).

The stories involving the women who came to Jesus and anointed him with oil are two different stories involving two different women (neither of which is Mary Magdalene). Matthew 26:6–13, Mark 14:3–9, and John 12:2–11 all speak of the same event involving Mary of Bethany at the home of Simon the leper, probably a leper who had been healed by Jesus and had become one of his followers. This event occurred in Bethany just days before the crucifixion, which is why Mary came to anoint Jesus for the event to come. 'She has come beforehand to anoint My body for burial' (Mark 14:8). Mary is never referred to as a sinner in any of the accounts of her. Nor does it say she was weeping.

On the other hand, Luke 7:36–50 speaks of the house of Simon the Pharisee rather than Simon the leper. This event occurred about a year before the crucifixion in the area around Galilee (Luke 7:1, 11). The woman here was forgiven of many sins. While Mary of Bethany possessed insight as to the upcoming death of Christ, the woman Luke describes had no such insight. She was there not to prepare Jesus for burial, which was still a year away, but simply to exhibit loving worship of the one who had forgiven her sins. There certainly are many similarities in these two events and those similarities have caused some to equate them, but they are clearly two different incidents involving two different women, in two different homes of men named Simon, in two different areas of the country, and occurring a year apart. It is important to make this distinction between them if we are to understand Mary of Bethany, who is never identified as a sinful woman.

In the following pages, we will look closely at the mysterious Mary of Bethany, a most unique and remarkable woman whose incredible faith, quiet spirit, and uncanny understanding of spiritual matters are a testimony to the power of God in the life of a woman totally committed to her Lord. Much has been written and taught about Mary and Martha, about Martha's busyness and Mary's adoration and worship. But there is more to Mary's story, much more. As we look closely at Mary's life, we will find her to be the perfect role model for women today, one whose amazing story deserves to be told and retold, as Jesus said, 'in memory of her.'

# I

# Memorial:
# the mystery of Mary

Like all good detectives, we solve the mystery that is Mary of Bethany by beginning with the clues found in the three short biblical accounts of her, beginning with the Mary and Martha episode and ending with her anointing of Jesus for burial. Interestingly, all three incidents occurred in about a six-month time period, the last six months of Jesus' life on earth. Over the next chapters, we are going to look at these incidents in depth, but we start with the final episode because it uncovers mysteries about this amazing woman and deep truths we often miss, all of which are revealed by the Lord Jesus himself. Then when we go back to the Mary and Martha incident, the true meaning of that opening event becomes clear. It is much more than the harried Martha fussing with the serving and Mary sitting at Jesus' feet.

We begin with a meal served at the house of Simon the leper. We know from John 12 that Jesus came into Bethany six days before the Passover, which would make it the day before Palm Sunday, and six days before his crucifixion as the ultimate Passover Lamb. But the meal described here occurred just days before the Passover (Mark 14:1–3), during Jesus' last week on earth. The occasion involved Martha, who was serving, and Lazarus, whose resurrection months earlier must have prompted many interesting conversations at that table! Mary was there as well, along with the disciples of Jesus. The incident is described in three of the Gospels, Matthew 26:6–13, Mark 14:3–9, and John 12:2–8, each one adding additional details and nuances.

Matthew 26:6–13 'And when Jesus was in Bethany at the house of Simon the leper, a woman came to Him having an alabaster flask of very costly fragrant oil, and she poured it on His head as he sat at the table. But when His disciples saw it, they were indignant, saying, "Why this waste? For this fragrant oil might have been sold for much and given to the poor." But when Jesus was aware of it, he said to them, "Why do you trouble the woman? For she has done a good work for Me. For you have the poor with you always, but Me you do not have always. For in pouring this fragrant oil on My body, she did it for My burial. Assuredly, I say to you, wherever this gospel is preached in the whole world, what this woman has done will also be told as a memorial to her."'

Mark 14:3–9 'And being in Bethany at the house of Simon the leper, as He sat at the table, a woman came having an alabaster flask of very costly oil of spikenard.

Then she broke the flask and poured it on His head. But there were some who were indignant among themselves, and said, "Why was this fragrant oil wasted? For it might have been sold for more than three hundred denarii and given to the poor." And they criticized her sharply. But Jesus said, "Let her alone. Why do you trouble her? She has done a good work for Me. For you have the poor with you always, and whenever you wish you may do them good; but Me you do not have always. She has done what she could. She has come beforehand to anoint My body for burial. Assuredly, I say to you, wherever this gospel is preached in the whole world, what this woman has done will also be told as a memorial to her.'"

John 12:1–8 'Then, six days before the Passover, Jesus came to Bethany, where Lazarus was who had been dead, whom He had raised from the dead. There they made Him a supper; and Martha served, but Lazarus was one of those who sat at the table with Him. Then Mary took a pound of very costly oil of spikenard, anointed the feet of Jesus, and wiped His feet with her hair. And the house was filled with the fragrance of the oil. But one of His disciples, Judas Iscariot, Simon's son, who would betray Him, said, "Why was this fragrant oil not sold for three hundred denarii and given to the poor?" This he said, not that he cared for the poor, but because he was a thief, and had the money box; and he used to take what was put in it. But Jesus said, "Let her alone; she has kept this for the day of My burial. For the poor you have with you always, but Me you do not have always."'

What woman would not want to hear such words of

praise from the Lord Jesus? We all long to hear him
say to us in that final day, 'Well done, good and faithful
servant.' And who would not want to be defended by
God incarnate when we are falsely accused? Jesus'
words of praise for Mary included, 'She has done a
good work to me' (Matthew 26:10; Mark 14:6), 'She did
what she could' (Mark 14:8), and the remarkable final
commendation: 'Wherever this gospel is preached in the
whole world, what this woman has done will also be told
as a memorial to her' (Matthew 26:13; Mark 14:9). What
an amazing statement! He promised Mary that she was
to be honored all over the world for all time. Did those
in attendance actually comprehend what he was saying?
Did Mary? What exactly did Mary do and for what was
Jesus commending her? And what was it about her 'good
work' that merited such memorializing?

## She has done a good work

There is no doubt that many Christian women today are
good workers. I offer the following portrait of a typical
Christian woman, especially in the West. She is in her
mid-thirties, married, with three children. She works
part time while her children are in school or perhaps
she home schools the younger ones while the older
one is in a 'good' school, perhaps a Christian or charter
school. She volunteers at the school regularly in order
to keep an eye on what goes on there and to continue
playing an important part in her kids' lives while they
are educated by people she doesn't really trust all that
much. She is involved with her church, especially the

children's ministry, and spends many Sundays in the nursery, volunteering to teach, or assisting the children's church teachers. She entertains as frequently as she can and makes every effort to have her home and table represent her and her family well.

Every evening she helps her kids with their homework, tries to have meaningful conversations with her husband, all while doing those endless chores that never seem to go away—cleaning, laundry, cooking. Weekends are given over to shopping for food, clothes and school supplies, always mindful of the budget which never seems to quite balance out, often leaving her with 'too much month at the end of the money.' In her spare time, she tries to work out and keep in shape, but spare hours seem to be elusive and when they do come, she's often too tired to do anything but talk on the phone, send a few texts, or update her Facebook page. After all, she really must keep in touch with her friends, and often finds their lives are pretty much like hers as they all multi-task their way through life.

As often as she can, she takes out her Bible or carves out 15–20 minutes in the morning for a 'quiet time', although her heart really isn't in it and she has little peace because she feels the pressure of all those tasks on her to-do list or her iPhone's calendar. So she says a quick prayer for her family, tosses down her morning jolt of caffeine, and charges into her day like a Thoroughbred out of the starting gate. Overall, she feels pretty good about all the things she can accomplish, but deep down inside there is a nagging doubt about the value of it all. She is committed to her family, but she sometimes wonders about the eternal significance of what she does, although she really doesn't have much time to ponder the eternal. Her reverie is interrupted by beeping appliances, ringing cell phones, barking dogs, squabbling kids, and the endless demands of others. Who has time for eternity? She's just trying to get through the next few hours.

By modern standards and compared to the multi-tasking Christian woman, Mary wasn't much of a worker. Yet, her simple act of preparing Jesus for burial was sufficient to gain acclaim for the ages. Seen through the eyes of the modern Christian woman, it hardly seems fair. Besides, if anyone should be commended, it's Martha, whose life was given over to service. What was so special about Mary's act? After all, it couldn't have taken more than a couple of minutes out of her day. What good work did she perform to earn such high praise from Jesus? We will explore this in depth in a later chapter, but suffice it to say that Mary's good work was not what we normally think of as working for the Lord.

## The work that is not work

Christians through the ages have suffered from a misconception, the idea that we may be justified by faith, but it's our work for the Lord that really counts. It's what distinguishes the spiritual giants from the rest of us. We would all agree that we are not saved by works, but once we're saved, by golly we had better get cracking! There is so much to do, so many people to witness to, so many causes demanding our time and money, so much serving to do! After all, faith without works is dead, isn't it?

Hard-wired into our DNA is the idea that what we do for Christ is just as important as what he did for us. Nothing could be farther from the truth. In fact, it's the very opposite of the gospel, the good news that Jesus not only paid it all, he also did it all. Every false religion throughout man's history distorts that biblical truth. I once wrote a series of articles for a Bible website on fifteen false religions. After about the first six or seven, I found myself writing the same thing over and over because all false religions have the same two things in common: all deny the deity of Christ and all teach some form of works salvation. Deep in the heart of all people is this nagging voice telling us we must *do something* to win God's favor. Even if we accept that we are saved by faith, and most Christians do accept it, we are still compelled to *do something* to add to that faith some kind of deeds.

This was Martha's mistake. Yes, she loved Jesus. She may have even believed he was the Messiah and wanted to show it by doing her very best for him. But she made a crucial error in not recognizing that what we believe is ultimately more important than what we do. Of course we are to engage in good works, because faith without works truly is dead faith, no faith at all. But good works are the *result* of salvation, not the cause of it. They flow from salvation and are the fruit of it. What we forget as we work ourselves to the bone trying to make everything right or perfect is that God has done it all. From beginning to end, the work is his. Ephesians 2:8–10 tells us that we are saved by *his* grace through the faith that *he* gives as a free gift and then we go forth to the good works that *he* has prepared for us and foreordained that we would do them. It's all of him, no matter how much we may want to think otherwise.

Many of the people who followed Jesus didn't understand this truth, as recorded in John 6:22–29. 'Then they said to Him, "What shall we do, that we may work the works of God?"' (v. 28). You see, the Jews of that day were familiar with the many requirements of the Law of Moses. They were expecting Jesus to reiterate those requirements or give them some additional ones. They wanted to know what works *they could do.* Jesus' answer must have shocked them. 'This is the work of God, that you believe in Him whom he sent' (v. 29). They were looking for a 'to-do list' of tasks and he said, in essence, there is nothing you can do. The only work is the work which God does, the *work of God.* They asked about the works (plural) that they could do. He replied that the only work (singular) was that which God himself does. God's work is that we believe in him. God's work is to give us the *gift* of faith that justifies us. The focus of faith in Scripture is always on what God has done for us, not on what we do for him.

Martha was concerned about doing *for Jesus.* Mary's concern was receiving *from Jesus.* This is the essence of works over faith. Works go toward God; faith comes from God. Once we start down the 'I have to do' road, we make the same mistake Martha made the first time we meet her. We allow the pressure over what we must do for Christ to overwhelm our gratitude for what he has done for us. What we often fail to grasp is that when we elevate good works over the priorities of faith and true worship, the good works themselves are spoiled and become that which draws us away from Christ, not toward him. Then the works become an end in themselves and when we achieve those ends, we can too easily begin to feel pretty good about ourselves. That leads to the pride that robs God of the glory that belongs only to him.

Martha's problem wasn't her attitude about the serving. It was her attitude about herself. Once the serving became her main concern, instead of the One whom she served, the focus shifted from Jesus to the manner in which she was, in her eyes, being ill-used. That ruined what began as a good work of service. Had she been able to serve the meal in simple gratitude for what Jesus had done for her, her service would have been acceptable to him and endeared her to him. As it was, it caused a rift between her and her sister and prompted from Jesus a mild, although loving, rebuke.

It was Mary who performed the ultimate good work, that which is born of total faith in Jesus—who he was and what he had revealed about his upcoming death. It was the kind of faith that rested entirely in God. Hers was a mind-blowing faith, an indomitable faith that crushes fears, doubts, and guilt like so many pebbles under a steamroller, an invincible faith for the ages, a rock solid, life-altering faith, a faith that is available to every one of us. Every Christian woman can have that kind of faith, even though it may seem impossible. Every woman can have the confidence and assurance that comes not from faith in ourselves, but in the One who created faith and who willingly bestows it. Mary's story is the story of that amazing faith, a story we miss because she says so little, but a story which was told by the Holy Spirit in Scripture and praised by the very lips of Jesus Christ himself.

In later chapters, we will explore the effects of Mary's faith and how it came about, the mystery of what she knew, how she knew it, and why she alone had the knowledge that others, especially the disciples, had missed. We will also look at Mary's response to criticism and how it differs from our own responses in the face of harsh words of disapproval from others. We will look at the peace that characterized her life and how it differed markedly from Martha's turmoil, and we will see how Jesus lovingly and patiently taught Martha the ways of peace so that in the end she mirrored Mary's tranquil heart and mind. Most importantly, we will understand how every Christian woman can have the same earth-shattering faith that characterized Mary's life and which can transform our lives in ways we never imagined.

To understand all these marvelous truths about Mary and how she came to be the woman she was, we have to turn back to our first contact with Mary and Martha in Luke 10 and to the events that led up to it.

## 2

# Mary and Martha:
# peace versus turmoil

To see the effects of Mary's incredible faith, we have to begin with the first time the Bible reveals her to us. We are all familiar with the story of Mary and Martha as told in Luke 10:38–42:

'Now it happened as they went that He entered a certain village; and a certain woman named Martha welcomed Him into her house. And she had a sister called Mary, who also sat at Jesus' feet and heard His word. But Martha was distracted with much serving, and she approached Him and said, "Lord, do You not care that my sister has left me to serve alone? Therefore tell her to help me." And Jesus answered and said to her, "Martha, Martha, you are worried and troubled about many things. But one thing is needed, and Mary has chosen that good part, which will not be taken away from her.'"

We know from John 11:1 that the 'certain village' is Bethany, a small town just two miles from Jerusalem in the southern part of Israel. But the story of Mary of Bethany begins years before we see her this first time at the feet of Jesus. This was certainly not the first time Mary, Martha, and Lazarus met Jesus. They were intimately familiar with him, who he was, and what he had done. This was no ordinary houseguest, but a cherished friend, whom they loved and who loved them. 'Now Jesus loved Martha and her sister and Lazarus' (John 11:5).

The Bible doesn't tell us specifically how or when Mary first came to know Jesus. This, too, is a mystery, but from his travels around the country, we can piece together the first two and a half years of his ministry and the many times their paths may have crossed. Perhaps Mary was introduced to Jesus through the ministry of John the Baptist who baptized at Bethabara, less than 20 miles from Bethany (John 1:28). She may have been one of the many who were baptized by John. Was she there the day Jesus came to John to be baptized and to 'fulfill all righteousness' (Matthew 3:15)? Did she, too, see the Spirit descending upon him like a dove and could she have heard the voice from heaven saying, 'This is My beloved Son, in whom I am well pleased'? (Matthew 3:16–17)

It could be that Mary and her siblings were among the multitudes in Jerusalem for the Passover when Jesus cleansed the Temple the first time, driving out the money-changers and shocking the religious leaders. John 2:23 records that 'many believed in His name when they saw the signs which He did.' Was Mary one of the many? When Jesus went north to the area around the Sea of Galilee to call his disciples, was Mary among the 'great multitudes [that] followed Him—from Galilee, and from Decapolis, Jerusalem, Judea, and beyond the Jordan' (Matthew 4:25)?

Each time Jesus returned to Jerusalem to celebrate the Passover and other feasts, he did incredible miracles, the likes of which had never been seen before. His reputation spread like wildfire in a culture where the only news media was word of mouth. We can picture Mary gathering with the other women at wells and market places in Bethany to hear stories of the amazing deeds done by Jesus.

Were Mary, Martha and Lazarus among the multitude from Judea described in Mark 3:7–8? We know the Pharisees followed him everywhere, accusing him of healing and casting out demons by the power of Satan. Did Mary hear these discussions and ponder them in her heart? Was she among the throngs who heard him preach the Sermon on the Mount and the Beatitudes?

In the end, we just don't know whether Mary was one of the multitudes who followed Jesus as he traveled up and down the country between Galilee and Judea, or if she and her brother and sister only met with him when he came to Judea. One thing we know for sure— by the time we first see Jesus and Mary together, she is fully convinced of his identity. She is there at his feet listening to the Word of her Lord, an act that was truly remarkable for a woman in that culture. A woman could learn in the back of the synagogue, in the women's section. But at his feet, Mary took the posture of ancient disciples and learners who sat at the feet of their teachers. Paul is described as being brought up 'at the feet of Gamaliel' (Acts 2:23), so this was a position well-known in that culture. But not for a woman. For her to take such a position was shocking. But this is not the last time we will see Mary putting herself at risk of criticism to be near Jesus.

By the time we first see Mary at Jesus' feet, she has already known him, possibly for nearly three years, and been known to him. Now he is in her home. He has graced her family with his presence, his love, his words of truth and wisdom. To Mary, the thought of being anywhere but at his feet would be unthinkable. It would be as if a king or a president came into a home today and the residents found some mundane task to perform instead of attending to his every word. Mary's position at his feet indicated her deep interest in Jesus' teaching, getting as close as she could in order to not miss a word, listening intensely to the most powerful, clear, truthful teacher who ever spoke.

There she is right alongside Jesus and enjoying the light of love in his eyes, not concerned about the perceptions of the men who may have been more comfortable with having her in the kitchen, although if they felt that way, they apparently kept it to themselves. If Jesus did not rebuke her or tell her to remember her place, surely they had no right to do so! But Mary wasn't concerned about conventions. Her concern was listening to the Lord, being as close to him as possible, drinking in every word, every nuance, every nugget of truth from his lips. Her priority was to hear, to listen, to love that truth, to believe it, to hide it in her heart, and to act on it. Every one of Mary's actions from this point on will reflect that priority.

Mary has often been criticized by women whose sympathies lie with Martha, and what woman doesn't identify with Martha? She was doing her best to prepare a meal for Jesus, her Lord whom she loved. Of course she wanted it to be perfect! Don't we all spend days in preparing our homes and the best meal we can whip up when we invite others in? Isn't that what hospitality is all about? We clean and shop and cook and make the best presentation possible because we want our guests to be comfortable, to enjoy their meal, and to feel that we value them enough to do our best for them. How much more can that be said when the guest is the Lord himself? What's wrong with what Martha did? Nothing, actually.

Jesus did not rebuke Martha for all she had done, for which he might even have been grateful. What grieved his heart was seeing Martha 'worried and troubled about many things' (Luke 10:41). We hear the concern in his voice as he addresses her: 'Martha, Martha.' His concern was not for the state of her home and table, but for the state of her soul and her heart. Martha was not a woman at peace, but the Prince of Peace began in this incident to teach Martha the way to true tranquility of mind and stillness of heart. We will see him continue those lessons in the next event in which they meet, and we will see the results of that education in the last episode.

## The woman of peace

The portrait of a typical Christian woman in chapter 1 shows her to be busy and engaged in many things, perhaps even 'worried and troubled' about many things. But she lacks a sense of peace. We all want to be women of peace, don't we? We want peace of mind, peace in our relationships, peace with God, and we want to be at peace with ourselves. But it seems that so many things conspire to rob us of the tranquility and calm that we seek. What is true peace, how do we get it, and why does it seem so hard to come by? Mary is the epitome of the woman at peace, while Martha seems to exemplify someone in turmoil.

Mary seems to have taken to heart the words of Psalm 46:10, 'Be still, and know that I am God.' How difficult it is for modern women to be still! The kind of stillness the psalmist speaks of isn't emptiness or laziness. Rather, it's resting in the sure knowledge of God—his nature, his character, his history of faithfulness, his perfect plan, and his sovereign power. It's the intentional forsaking of frivolous activity, a letting go of self-effort, and a reevaluation of ourselves, our abilities, and our endless spiritual to-do lists. It is Mary who is still and committed to knowing God. It is Martha who cannot be still for a moment, not even to attend to the words of God in flesh. Martha is not a woman at peace and, as with all women in turmoil, her lack of peace is evidenced in her speech.

The woman at peace usually is a woman who doesn't speak all that much and when she does, she speaks words of depth, words of encouragement, words of praise and peace. Our first encounter with Martha sees her speaking words of accusation ('Don't you care!?'), words of complaint ('My sister has left me to serve all alone!'), and an order ('Tell her to help me!'). And notice, too, the emphasis on self: 'my sister has left ME … ' 'Tell her to help ME!' Here is an amazing scene—a harried, frustrated woman reproaching and bossing around the Creator of the universe, God incarnate. We can only marvel at his patience and loving kindness toward her. Of course he cared, and deep down, she must have known that. Several times in the Gospels, we are told that he loved Lazarus and his sisters. But the pressure of presenting herself, her home, and her meal in their very best light got the best of her reasoning and her emotions took over. This is why Jesus rebuked her gently, not to make her feel even worse, but to reason with her out of love and concern for her. Of course he cared, but his care was for her, not for what she could do, not for her efforts, and not for the many things she was concerned with. As Christian women, we are blessed with that same care and attention from our Lord, care for the state of our souls and concern for the peace in our hearts. Oh, if only we knew him well enough to truly believe that. What peace would be the result!

Martha's care about 'many things' and the turmoil that resulted from it remind us that misplaced priorities often lead to strife and contention in families. For example, the woman who insists her home must be spotless at all times can make the home seem like a sterile museum to those who must tread with care lest they spill something, leave something out of place, or neglect a chore. Such a woman can appear unreasonable and overbearing in the eyes of family members, and the home can be seen a place of constant duties instead of the refuge from the cares of the world it is designed to be. Worse, she can give the distinct impression of caring more for the kitchen counters or dining room table than for the interests and feelings of her husband and children. Though she may envision herself as a 'domestic goddess,' she runs the danger of being seen as a domestic tyrant by loved ones. Of course family members should be involved in caring for the home, but the woman who allows materialistic worldliness to produce a distorted view of her home can turn it into a place of friction and disharmony.

Mary is a woman at peace, a serenity born of knowing God and making him her priority. In direct contrast to Martha, Mary says nothing. No self-defense, no retaliation against her sister, no accusations of her own, nothing. Her silence speaks volumes to women today. Martha is often depicted as the practical one and Mary the emotional one, but the text indicates the exact opposite. Women whose emotions are controlling them are the ones running around spewing forth verbally everything in their hearts. Martha's negative emotions were on display—worry, frustration, peevishness—and, like all women, those emotions poured forth verbally. 'Out of the abundance of the heart, the mouth speaks,' Luke 6:45 reminds us. Women with the peace of God in their hearts are not exercising their tongues every second because their negative emotionality is reined in by the presence of the gifts of the Spirit and the positive emotions he produces, especially love, joy and peace. The tranquility in Mary's heart was evident in her actions, her lack of verbal outpourings, and her single-mindedness of purpose.

As women, our emotional nature tends to gush forth in our words. Women's verbal skills begin to appear early in life. Studies of children's behavior have found that girls speak earlier, have larger vocabularies, and are better at spelling and reading. Combine that with our emotional nature and the part of the curse that causes us to try to control others and you have Martha. A woman in the throes of emotional turmoil is generally not going to be a silent woman. Even if external forces oblige us to keep our mouths closed, the emotional monologue runs in our minds nonstop. We are women of words, not women of silence, and the culture encourages us to babble and gush forth every thought that comes into our heads, no matter how silly, inane, or self-serving those thoughts might be. We are addicted to expressing ourselves, and a myriad of avenues in which to do so exist—Facebook, Twitter, cell phones, texting, blogs, call-in shows, you name it. And have you noticed that in our churches, our small groups are less and less about sound Bible teaching and more about everyone having their say? Less and less about the person of Christ and more about what we think and feel? Has any of this helped to bring about strong, confident Christian women with peaceful hearts and minds? If we're honest, we have to say no.

## The search for peace

We have to admit that most Christian women identify much more with Martha than they do with Mary. That's because we don't really understand that our lack of peace comes from seeking peace through avenues other than those clearly laid out in Scripture. Jesus and the apostle Paul had a good deal to say about peace. For one thing, peace is one of the fruits of the Spirit (Galatians 5:22). That means peace is not something we concoct on our own. It comes to us in a package deal from the Holy Spirit given to all who belong to God through faith in Jesus Christ.

So the first step in the pursuit of peace is to have a reasonable assurance of our salvation. Paul exhorts us to examine ourselves to see if we are truly in the faith, to test ourselves (2 Corinthians 13:5). If we don't have that confidence, we are to ask for it because God has promised to assure us. Romans 8:16 tells us that 'the Spirit Himself bears witness with our spirit that we are children of God,' which means the very same Holy Spirit who gives us peace as one of his gifts also gives us the inner conviction that we belong to him. Anyone whose life is characterized by a lack of peace should begin by praying for the indwelling of the Spirit, the certainty he provides, and the gifts he promises.

Too often we look for a sense of worldly peace instead of the peace which is only available through Christ. We fall for the lie that says personal peace is obtained by financial security, professional respect in our chosen field, and family success. Our minds are filled with 'if onlys' that promise peace in our hearts and minds. *If only* we could pay off all our debts and have a fat savings account, then we could be comfortable. *If only* I could get that new job, juicy promotion, advanced degree, etc., then I could relax. *If only* the kids would do well in school, get into good colleges, begin successful careers and marry the right person, then all would be well. But these are just more lies from the controller of the culture, Satan, whose goal is to get us to focus our minds on ourselves and the puny rewards the world offers, none of which satisfy or provide the inner peace we seek.

But Jesus promised an entirely different peace, 'Peace I leave with you, My peace I give to you; *not as the world gives do I give to you.* Let not your heart be troubled, neither let it be afraid' (John 14:27, emphasis added). His is the only true peace, the peace that Mary found, the peace which guarded her heart and mind through Christ (Philippians 4:7). She had peace *in Christ*, not in herself or in what the world has to offer. Jesus promised that we, too, could have that peace in him: 'These things I have spoken to you, that *in Me you may have peace.* In the world you will have tribulation; but be of good cheer, I have overcome the world' (John 16:33, emphasis added).

There is no possible way for the things of this world to truly satisfy a Christian and give her peace. No amount of money, prestige, comfort, education, health, wealth or prosperity can provide the peace only Christ affords. His is an eternal kingdom which provides for its citizens the hope of heaven and a life on earth characterized by the kind of peaceful heart Mary exhibited. 'For the kingdom of God is not eating and drinking, but righteousness and peace and joy in the Holy Spirit' (Romans 14:17). And the miraculous truth is that this same kingdom, this same peace and joy, is every bit as possible for us today as it was for Mary over 2000 years ago. If we pattern our lives after Mary, if we become women who seek the one 'needful' thing, we will see our lives transformed.

This is the lesson that Martha finally learned. We will look at this in depth in another chapter, but Martha gets some serious lessons on living in peace. The second time we see the sisters, Martha is still pouring forth words to the Lord, while Mary sits quietly, peacefully waiting for the Master's call. When she receives that call, she rushes to him, falls at his feet and utters the only thing Scripture records her as saying, an affirmation of his deity. The third time we see them, Martha and Mary are both silent. Martha is still serving, but this time with a peaceful spirit, and Mary worships in faith, humility and peaceful silence. Martha's is the ultimate makeover, made new by the 'peace of God that passes all understanding' (Philippians 4:7).

# 3

# At Jesus' feet:
# hearing a word from the Lord

One of the mysteries of Mary is the question of just exactly how Mary became this woman of a peaceful heart while Martha was in turmoil. The first clue lies in Luke 10:39–40a: 'And she had a sister called Mary, who also sat at Jesus' feet and heard his word. But Martha was distracted with much serving.' Here is the description of two sisters, one sitting and listening and the other one doing. It's so hard for us to hear when we are busy doing. I can multi-task with the best of women, but one thing I cannot do is give my attention to conversation when I am engaged in some kind of activity. That's why I can't have someone in my kitchen talking to me as I prepare a meal. It's also why I can't write when my husband sits down in my office and starts telling me about his day. I can listen, or I can do. But not both.

Martha was busy doing and she was 'distracted' by her activity. Distracted from what? From listening to what was being said by Jesus. The Greek word for 'hear' in the Bible has two different uses. One denotes receiving sound with the sense of hearing. The other means to actually understand what is being heard. My cats sit on my lap while the TV is on and their ears receive the sound waves, but clearly they do not understand any of the content of those sound waves. How often do we sit in church or Bible studies while the words of the speakers wash over our ears, not penetrating our minds and hearts because we are distracted? Mary was hearing Jesus' word, listening to the very voice of God incarnate, and understanding what he was saying. We'll see the results of this kind of listening later on when she proves that she heard the same thing the disciples heard about Jesus' upcoming death, but she actually understood it, while they did not.

No doubt Martha could hear the words Jesus spoke as she was bustling around the house. After all, houses in Palestine in those days weren't the split-level, multi-room houses we have today in the West. Surely she heard the words of Jesus' teaching. But there is 'hearing' and there is 'listening,' two entirely different things. Martha may have heard, in the same way we hear background noise in restaurants or stores, but we really don't listen to it because we are attending to shopping or eating or table conversation. But Mary was actually listening to Jesus, attending to the words of life coming from him. There was no activity, no effort being expended on her part except the effort involved with taking in truth and meditating on it.

## Hearing from God

There is much written and spoken of today about hearing the voice of God, but what does it really mean to 'hear' God's voice? At the time of this book's writing, the marketing for a very popular book for Christian women says that the author 'decided to listen to God with pen in hand, writing down whatever she believed he was saying to her.' This concept of hearing 'a word from the Lord' has become very popular in Christian circles, at least in the U.S. I can't speak for the Brits or Europeans, but American Christian women are fascinated, some obsessively so, with the idea of God speaking to them personally. They journal about the thoughts they believe are coming from God. When a thought comes into their heads, especially if it relates to God's love and how much he longs for them and wants the best for them, they seize on that thought, attribute it to God, write it in their journals, and go about their day feeling good about having given God the chance to speak to them. But does God really speak to us this way? And how can we know for sure? There are many pitfalls inherent in seeking this type of communication, and we must be aware of them in order to keep from being deceived.

First and foremost, seeking to receive extra-biblical revelations from God and writing down what we think he is saying to us circumvents his stated method of communicating with his children. We hear from him through his Word and he hears from us through prayer. Hearing from him through any other means denies one of the basic foundational doctrines of the Christian faith—the sufficiency of Scripture, as recorded in 2 Timothy 3:16–17: 'All Scripture is given by inspiration of God, and is profitable for doctrine, for reproof, for correction, for instruction in righteousness, that the man [or woman] of God may be complete ('perfect' KJV), thoroughly equipped for every good work.' To believe we need a revelation from God in addition to the perfect, closed canon of Scripture is to deny that the Bible is sufficient to make us complete, thereby contradicting God. Do we really want to do that? If the Word is sufficient to make us complete, perfect and thoroughly equipped for every good work, what more is there to add?

The words 'thoroughly' and 'every' do not allow for gradations. In other words, there are no degrees of these words. Thoroughly means just that. We can't say that we are *partially* thoroughly equipped by the Word and need more words from God to make us *completely* thoroughly equipped. Nor can we say we are only equipped for *most* good works, but need more from God to prepare us for *every* good work. It's like trying to say one is somewhat pregnant. Either one is pregnant or she is not. So either the Bible is all we need, or we need something more from God. If we believe we need more than the Word, we contradict what God has already revealed to us. Why would we expect him to reveal more?

*Oh, but we must always verify what we hear from him by comparing it to Scripture!* That's the mantra of all who sincerely believe they are hearing extra-biblical revelations from God. There are two problems with that idea. First, the level of scriptural ignorance in today's churches is staggering, so much so that very few people are even capable of comparing what they think they are hearing to the Word. A perfect example is the saga of Angelica Zambrano, the Ecuadorian teenage girl who claimed that she was dead for 23 hours, during which time she met Jesus Christ who led her through hell and heaven so that she would be able to, in her words, 'come back and warn people' about the realities of the next life. She was hailed as a prophetess in a large part of the Christian world, both Catholic and Protestant. If those who accepted her as such had really been familiar with Scripture, they would have known that the idea of Jesus leading someone through heaven and hell so that they could come back and warn people directly contradicts what is revealed in the Bible. Jesus was very clear in the final statement of the story of the rich man and Lazarus: 'If they do not listen to Moses and the Prophets, they will not be convinced even if someone rises from the dead' (Luke 16:31). If Jesus said people would not be convinced by someone coming back from the grave, then never in a million years would he take a teenage girl on a quick tour of heaven and hell in order to do the very thing he has declared would be ineffective. Jesus didn't appear to this girl, no matter how sincerely she believes she heard from him. Those who accepted her testimony as true were not able, or not willing, to verify it scripturally.

The second problem with trying to verify extra-biblical

revelation with the Bible is that the one Scripture it's impossible to verify it by is 2 Timothy 3:16–17. We've already seen the inconsistency of believing the Bible is all we need and then asking for more revelations from God. In addition, 2 Peter 1:3 clearly states that 'His divine power has given to us all things that pertain to life and godliness, through the knowledge of Him who called us by glory and virtue,' that knowledge being obtained through only one source—his Word. If we tend to believe in extra-biblical revelations, those two concepts should really stop us in our tracks right there, shouldn't they?

Another pitfall in 'hearing a word from the Lord' is the implication of making such a statement. Remember the book marketing I mentioned earlier? The author was writing down what God was saying *to her*, as though he had something unique to say to her and her alone, something new that has never been revealed to anyone before. But if God is truly speaking to you, then you are on a level with the writers of Scripture and everything you write down is Scripture! If we were to try to add to the existing pages of the Bible every revelation and word from the Lord being heard by women today, the book would be so huge that we would each need a wheelbarrow to carry it around. We must be extremely careful about attempting to add anything to the revealed Word of God. Revelation 22:18 warns us, 'For I testify to everyone who hears the words of the prophecy of this book: If anyone adds to these things, God will add to him the plagues that are written in this book.' Whether that verse refers to the entire Bible or just the book of Revelation, the warning is the same: don't do it.

Finally, the thing that should make us uncomfortable with the idea of dialoguing with God is the inherent 'chumminess' of it all. If we imagine God sitting across the table entering into a dialogue with us, that automatically brings him down to our level and it becomes too easy, in our own minds, to see ourselves on his level. This is part of fallen human nature, inherited from Adam and Eve—the desire to be like God which is at the core of all sin, all deception, and all error. When Satan said to Eve that eating the fruit would make her like God (Gen. 3:15), she found that prospect irresistible. And, unlike us, Eve didn't even have a sin nature! We must beware of anything that puts us on the same level with God, in any way, shape or form, because it appeals to the part of all fallen men and women that desires equality with God.

Did Mary of Bethany dialog with God incarnate? She did not. Was she sitting at the table with him in a position of equality? She was not. She sat at his feet, the only truly appropriate place for all believers. In fact, all three episodes involving Mary find her in the same place each time, at Jesus' feet. We must remember that it was Mary who received the extraordinary commendation of the Lord Jesus himself and pattern ourselves after her, not after the authors of books encouraging us to enter into chats with the holy, incomparable Creator of the universe whose 'thoughts are higher than our thoughts' (Isaiah 55:8–9). 'Oh, the depth of the riches both of the wisdom and knowledge of God! How unsearchable are

His judgments and His ways past finding out! For who has known the mind of the Lord? Or who has become His counselor?' (Romans 11:33–34).

If this seems a too-harsh indictment of women who wish to dialog with God, it must be remembered that Satan approached Eve, not Adam (1 Timothy 2:14), and since that day, part of being the 'weaker vessel' (1 Peter 3:7) involves our gullibility and the lack of discernment born of an emotional nature. Those same qualities of vulnerability and emotionality create the danger of opening ourselves up to deceiving spirits, who can appear as angels of light (2 Corinthians 11:14) and whose sole desire is the destruction of our souls. We must be ever on guard against the 'roaring lion seeking whom he may devour' (1 Peter 5:8) and not give him an entryway into our minds. Demonic forces can whisper in the ears of the unsuspecting woman who desires to hear from God in an avenue other than the one he has ordained. Psalm 19:7–9 describes the Word of God: 'The law of the Lord is perfect, converting the soul; The testimony of the Lord is sure, making wise the simple; The statutes of the Lord are right, rejoicing the heart; The commandment of the Lord is pure, enlightening the eyes; The fear of the Lord is clean, enduring forever; The judgments of the Lord are true and righteous altogether.' Really, what more is there to add?

## Ears to hear: who had them, who didn't and how do we get them?

There is no doubt that God alone gives ears to hear, eyes

to see and a heart to understand his truth (Proverbs 20:12). There is simply no way to discern spiritual truth on our own. In considering Mary of Bethany's actions, it is clear that she had ears to hear and a heart to understand, whereas the disciples, in many instances, did not. Jesus frequently chided the disciples for not having ears to hear, for not understanding what he was saying. Why does God sometimes withhold ears to hear or the eyes of understanding? In both the Old and New Testaments, God declares three reasons why people do not have ears to hear and all are instructive for us today.

*We don't respond to what he has already revealed.* The Israelites saw the power of the Lord revealed to them in great signs and wonders. They watched in awe as he leveled plague after plague on Egypt until Pharaoh finally relented and freed them. They gazed upon his miraculous power as he parted the Red Sea for their escape from Egypt, drowning Pharaoh's army who were pursuing them. Then they experienced his leading for forty years in the desert while their clothes and shoes did not wear out and he provided food from heaven for them to eat. Although they saw these miracles with their bodily eyes, because of their disobedience, God withheld from them eyes and ears of understanding. The people were unable to achieve spiritual understanding because they did not feel the need of it, nor did they ask for it (Deuteronomy 29:1–6).

Several times after Jesus had finished illustrating truth through parables, he told the disciples 'He who has ears, let him hear.' After explaining the parables of the Seed and the Sower and the lampstand, he added, 'to you who hear, more will be given' (Mark 4:24). When we learn spiritual truth, apply it and seek more of it, we will receive more to understand and apply. However, if we do not value that which he has given us, even that 'will be taken away' (v. 25). The meaning to us is clear. As believers, we come to Christ as empty vessels, hungry and thirsty for Truth and for the presence of God in our lives, and we desire more and more of that which only he imparts. But over time, we can become dull to the things of the Spirit, and the cares of this world can choke out our desire for the sacred. We forget that we died with Christ and we neglect to set our minds 'on things above, not on things on the earth' (Colossians 3:2). The ears to hear, which we had at first, become tuned in to the frequencies of the culture, and before long we find there is too much cultural static to hear that which is coming from Christ. If we continue in that mode, we no longer respond to the spiritual truths which used to thrill us, and they become vague and indistinct as they are withdrawn from us. We allow worldly ideas and pleasures to corrupt and influence us, instead of letting the Word of Christ dwell in us richly (Colossians 3:16). If we don't respond to what we have already received, we can hardly expect God to give us more.

*What has been revealed doesn't line up with what we want.* One of the reasons the disciples did not understand much of what Jesus was saying is that they had expectations based on their own plans and ideas. Specifically, they were convinced Jesus had come to expel the Romans from Israel and set up his kingdom on earth then and there (Luke 19:11). They didn't understand much of what he said about God's plan of redemption and salvation which involved his death on the cross. In fact, the first time he revealed that the plan was to go to Jerusalem, be killed and raised the third day, Peter took him aside and rebuked him: 'Far be it from You, Lord; this shall not happen to You!' Jesus recognized who was influencing Peter and diagnosed the problem, saying to Peter, 'Get behind Me, Satan! You are an offense to Me, for you are not mindful of the things of God, but the things of men' (Matthew 16:21–23). Being mindful of 'the things of men' involves attending to the voice of our own understanding, our own desires and our own plans. When that voice drowns out the words of the Scriptures, we fail to understand what is really true and our spiritual hearing becomes dulled. But if we can say and truly mean, 'Your will, not mine, be done,' we will find our ears will open to his will in a miraculous way.

*We are disobedient.* The Israelites were warned by the prophet Ezekiel that their rebellious disobedience would result in their captivity and the withdrawing of God's protection from them. 'Now the word of the LORD came to me, saying: "Son of man, you dwell in the midst of a rebellious house, which has eyes to see but does not see, and ears to hear but does not hear; for they are a rebellious house"' (Ezekiel 12:1). It goes without saying that those in rebellion against God will not have the ears of understanding. Of course we all sin, but the rebellious woman is one who sins willfully and knowingly. Such a lifestyle will never lead to wisdom and understanding.

## Mary had ears to hear

We know that Mary sat at Jesus' feet hearing his words, but what was going through her mind at the time can only be a matter of speculation. What we do know is that she responded to what he revealed about his upcoming death and resurrection with the ears of understanding. The last time we see Mary, she is anointing him for his death and burial with expensive perfumed oil she had kept for that very occasion. We will explore this in depth in a later chapter, but she alone had ears to hear his words about the fate that lay before him. We also know that she was obedient to his call on the day of Lazarus's funeral, rising 'quickly' and going to him as soon as he summoned her (John 11:29). Mary exhibited a heart dedicated to obeying and serving her Lord as demonstrated by her place at his feet with the eyes and ears of understanding tuned to him, and she enjoyed the benefits God always gives to the woman whose heart is similarly inclined.

But make no mistake about it; such an inclination does not come naturally. Our natural preference is to listen to our own voices, our own feelings, and our own desires. Like faith itself, ears to hear life-changing spiritual truth is a gift from God. Clearly if our lives are characterized by the things that hinder ears to hear, that gift will not be forthcoming. But if we can truly say in prayer that our desire is to hear and understand truth, even if it may contradict the inclination of our natural hearts, God will not withhold it from us. When we delight in him, God has promised to give us the desire of our hearts (Psalm

37:4), meaning that he will place his desires into our hearts and then fulfill those desires. He seeks women who, like Mary, have hearts bent toward him and who desire their eyes and ears to be opened.

# 4

# Choosing the better:
# life choices

As I sit at my computer, I know the operating system is making many choices for me—filtering out harmful viruses, tuning up the system, automatically saving some things and deleting others, suggesting words and phrases as I type, identifying misspellings and grammar errors. Oh, that we could have such a reliable machine making all our personal choices for us! From the moment we rise in the morning, we make one choice after another. What to wear, what to eat, what to say, where to go, who to deal with, even how to think about things. As women who multi-task through life, we make thousands of conscious and unconscious choices, moment by moment, day by day, week after week, year in and year out. Something in our brains operates like the computer, leading us to choose for some things and against others. Each choice leads to an experience and each experience leads to a further choice and so on. Sometimes we make terrible choices that lead to disasters, both major and minor, and sometimes we, like Mary, choose what Jesus called 'the better,' the one thing that is needful, necessary, *the good part.*

Choosing the better is not limited to our quiet times and Sunday services, sitting and learning of Jesus, hearing his words and worshiping him. It's all those little decisions we make from day to day, decisions that can have consequences far beyond the moment. But what influences our decision-making process is very much like the operating system of the computer. What has been programmed into it causes it to act in a certain way and affects the eventual output. As the saying goes about computer operating systems, 'garbage in, garbage out.' The same is true for our minds, the operating systems of our lives. Everything we put into our minds, everything we hear, see, and read has an effect on what comes out in the form of words, actions and decisions. Each experience influences the next experience and each decision impacts the next one.

As we've noted before, Mary's experiences prior to the first time we see her at Jesus' feet influenced her to choose the course of action that Jesus said was better than what Martha chose. She knew that the Messiah himself sat in her house, the one who had healed the diseases of many, raised the dead, fed thousands from a few fish and loaves, and spoke with words of wisdom unlike any man before him. She took all those words and experiences, input them into her mental hard drive, processed them, and made the right decision that doing anything other than drinking in his every word was unthinkable. She knew that this rare opportunity was too rich and too critical to turn to anything else.

Mary made a conscious choice to sit at Jesus' feet in the same way that Martha made a conscious choice to serve. But worship is always a higher service to Christ than anything done on his behalf. Even those who love the Lord dearly can become so wrapped up in doing things for Christ that we cease to hear from him and lose sight of what *he has done for us*. We must never allow our service for Christ to become more important than our worship of him. If we do, then the works become an end in themselves, and the result is the temptation to exalt the self and depreciate the work of Christ on our behalf. Simply put, it's not about what we can and should do for him; it's about what he has already done for us. But the tendency among so many Christians is to do more, work harder, and serve more. Sadly, many churches promote that mindset, elevating good deeds over sound doctrine and true worship. When that happens, we become like Martha, 'distracted' by the works we perform. We can lose our perspective about the cross and allow the anxiety over what we feel we must do for Christ to override our thankfulness to him for what he has finished on the cross.

Mary's choice of the better came out of a heart conditioned by what she knew from having ears to hear and the eyes of understanding. Jesus commended her for that choice, noting that it would 'not be taken away from her,' and he reminded Martha that what Mary had chosen was the one thing she truly needed. Some have suggested that, in this statement, Jesus was saying Martha should have simplified her meal planning and that only one dish was needed, rather than an elaborate meal of many dishes. But that contradicts the text. If he meant one dish of food was needed, how could that not be taken away from Mary? No, the context makes it clear that the one needful thing was Mary's chosen course of action, that which was timeless and everlasting. Food for the body is temporary and fleeting; food for the soul is eternal. Mary chose to feed her soul with the bread of life and the result of the choices she made produced in her a peace that Martha lacked, as well as an uncanny understanding of spiritual truth that the disciples lacked.

## What influences our choices?

Understanding the factors that influence our choices can help us recognize when we are being negatively influenced to make bad decisions and help us avoid doing and saying things that ultimately hurt us. In the same way, we need to know how to develop and strengthen within our own minds and hearts that which produces peace and harmony. One of the strongest pulls on our decision-making process is the opinions of others and the pressure those opinions exert upon us. We all want to be liked and accepted by those in our immediate circle. We even desire the good opinion of the world in general. No one wants to be seen in a negative light. The impact of peer pressure and the importance of social influence cannot be overstated. The popularity of social media attests to the pull that is exerted by the desire for the good opinions of others, the need to be connected with others in a positive manner. What we sometimes fail to understand is that 'all who desire to live godly in Christ Jesus will suffer persecution' (2 Timothy 3:12). If we take a clear stand for godliness, we simply have to expect that some will be offended by it, no matter how innocently we act or how lovingly we speak. Jesus promised that we would be hated for his sake, but in our world of intense social interactions, we resist the idea of even being seen in a negative light, much less being hated. No one wants to be persecuted, so we often tailor our choices to move us along on the path of least resistance.

We can only imagine how much Mary wanted to be loved and accepted by her family and the disciples of Jesus who were welcomed into her home. Here were men who followed the Savior she adored, who lived with him and whom he called 'brothers.' Surely she wanted to be seen by them in a positive light. Yet she defied the socially accepted convention of the day that required women to remain in the kitchen or in the back of the synagogue. She must have known her actions could incur their disapproval, whether they expressed it or not. She must have felt their questioning stares. Perhaps a certain chill filled the room. Certainly Martha's reaction was negative. But Mary's choice at that moment was to risk the approval of those who meant much to her in order to obtain the peace and joy at the feet of the One who meant the most to her. She was compelled from within to make a choice against the prevailing conventions of the day, to risk the regard of the men in attendance and even invite the displeasure of a beloved sister—all to obtain that which could never be taken away from her. What she knew, and what we need to grasp today, is that the good opinions of others are fleeting and unstable, but the good opinion of the Lord is precious and eternal.

The only way we can make these types of choices in our own lives is to do what Mary did—fill our minds and hearts with the knowledge of God, become so intimately acquainted with him that we feel his very presence in our decision-making moments. Even the most timid of women can become giants of strength and fearlessness as we are reminded in Daniel 11:32, 'the people who know their God shall be strong, and carry out great exploits.' For women who are terrified that someone might think negatively of them, risking the good opinions of others can be the greatest exploit in their lives. But making the choice to stand for godliness in an increasingly ungodly world will always be difficult. At least we don't have to face the same fates as the prophets and apostles when we refuse to go along with the crowd and stand alone for Christ. We won't be boiled in oil, beheaded, crucified or sawn in half as some of them were. For the sensitive woman, however, sometimes the cold shoulder and rolling eyes of her friends can pierce her heart as painfully as any Roman sword. But if our hearts are filled with the truth of the Scriptures and love of Jesus, we will be compelled to make the choice to risk it all for him, as Mary did.

Another strong influence on our decision making

is the culture in which we live, especially in the West. A huge part of marketing is the psychological study of how consumers make decisions and what types of information affects our decisions. Big money is invested in the effort to sway our choices in everything we buy and consume, from food and clothing to entertainment. Not one of our marketplace decisions is made entirely free from the influence of marketing, whether we recognize it or not. At the bottom of all marketing ploys is the plan to make us feel good about choosing certain products, eating certain foods, watching or listening to certain entertainments. Even if the Spirit of God who lives within us sets off an alarm bell about some part of the product or experience we are considering, the pull of that which appeals to our human senses can cause us to suppress it. For women, that pull usually involves an appeal to the emotions.

For example, we have all watched a movie or video and felt uncomfortable about some of the scenes or the language, only to have that discomfort outweighed by its appeal to our romantic natures. Sure there are scenes and language of a sexual nature, but the guy and girl are so cute and they end up together, don't they? That makes it alright. The culture, which is ultimately controlled by Satan, knows how to coat the poison with just enough chocolate to make it appealing. But each time we stifle the voice of our consciences in order to enjoy the romantic moment, we have made the decision to do just a little more to deaden our minds, dull our senses, and poison our spirits.

The first step in making good choices in the culture

we live in is to pray for the discernment to recognize the influence of demonic forces in that culture and for the conviction that we simply must distance ourselves from it. As the apostle John reminded those of his day, 'we know that we are of God, and the whole world lies under the sway of the wicked one' (1 John 5:19). We can't choose to live with one foot in the world and one in the kingdom of God without serious consequences. 'Do you not know that friendship with the world is enmity with God? Whoever therefore wants to be a friend of the world makes himself an enemy of God' (James 4:4). No woman would make the conscious choice to be an enemy of God. Why, then, do we so often allow the culture to influence us to do just that? The answer is that Satan's culture is subtly geared to dull our minds to the consequences of our choices and decisions. That's why it is so important to pray for and rely on the power of the Spirit to guide our choices and to listen to him when he pulls on our hearts. Recognizing and rejecting evil, no matter how prettily wrapped the package it comes in, becomes easier each time we do it. Conversely, giving in to evil becomes easier, and the evil harder to resist, each time we make the wrong choice to follow the culture's dictates.

Past experience is another influence in the decision making process. Faced with a choice we have made before, we naturally think back to that experience and gauge whether or not to make the same choice based on the previous outcomes. This is how children learn to keep their hands off the hot stove, to refrain from pulling the cat's tail, and avoid antagonizing an older and stronger child on the playground. Clearly, in these cases choosing the better thing is obvious. As we mature, however, choosing the better gets a little more complicated, especially when it involves the spiritual. If standing up for what is right in the past has caused us to lose friends, alienate family members, or be passed over for job promotions, we are less likely to take the same risk without some serious contemplation of the possible outcome. Even in the Christian world, those who stand for a literal interpretation of Scripture or who hold to truths such as an eternal hell, Jesus as the only way to God, or the sovereignty of God in salvation, can find themselves ostracized and reticent to express themselves openly. Painful past experiences with the negative reactions of others can tempt even mature Christians to mute their most strongly-held convictions.

For women, strong emotions such as fear and guilt can be huge factors in making choices and decisions. Women fear the loss of relationships, illness and death of loved ones, the aging process and loss of attractiveness. These fears can cause us to lose perspective and make unwise choices and decisions. A woman who fears losing the love and respect of her husband may become clingy, possessive or suspicious. Without a secure hold on her worth in the eyes of the God who loves her, she may make foolish and desperate choices that lead to further insecurity. Irrational fears can cause mothers to make wrong choices involving their children. They refuse to let their children out of their sight, become overbearing and overly solicitous, and refuse to let them grow and mature, all due to an inadequate understanding of the sovereignty of God in all things. Fear of aging and losing feminine charm can lead to unwise lifestyle choices such as unhealthy dieting, perpetual shopping and the endless search for the perfect cosmetic that will turn back the clock. These are often unconscious choices, but all are born out of a lack of the kind of secure knowledge of God, his nature, and his plans that Mary possessed.

Irrational feelings of guilt are also the motivator of many bad choices. The overly guilt-ridden woman can make choices based on the conviction that she is responsible for all family conflicts and is at fault when things go wrong in the lives of loved ones. She feels tremendous pressure to do all in her power to make everyone happy and when that doesn't happen, she feels responsible and the guilt can become unbearable. This leads to more bad choices and on and on. What she doesn't truly understand is 'there is now no condemnation for those in Christ Jesus' (Romans 8:1), none. Mary seemed to have grasped this important truth. If Jesus didn't condemn her for her actions, she had no reason to allow guilt to cause her to forego choosing the better course of action, staying at his feet and, later, anointing him for burial, despite Martha's and the disciples' objections. Fear and guilt can be tremendously powerful motivators in our decision-making process, but far more powerful is God's truth when it permeates our thoughts and feelings. No negative emotion can withstand that power.

## The good part

By telling Martha that Mary had 'chosen that good part,' Jesus was saying that some things are better than others, and some choices are wiser and more beneficial than others. This is certainly as true today in the lives of women as it was in Bethany all those years ago. What Mary chose that day was Christ himself, the substance of his words, the nearness of his person, and the gifts only he can offer: peace, joy, comfort, and eternal salvation. The same choice presents itself to each of us today. God himself is said to be the good part, the portion of his people in Psalm 73:26, 'My flesh and my heart fail; But God is the strength of my heart and my portion forever.' The psalmist, in referring to his flesh and heart, is comparing the earthly life to true eternal life he has found in God. By choosing the eternal, as Mary did, we choose that which cannot be taken away from us because it is has no end. Martha's choice would be taken from her, for her services would die with her; Mary's choice would never be taken away, being spiritual and eternal. It is the 'one thing' we need; all else is as a puff of wind.

Martha must have been able to hear Jesus as she worked. But as noted, being able to hear is not the same as listening. In the same way that Martha's busyness hampered her ability to comprehend spiritual truth, the modern woman's ears are so often clogged by the extraneous that we, too, lose the ability to perceive that which cannot be taken away from us. We can sit in church and hear the words of a sermon, but unless the meaning and truth in that sermon penetrate into our hearts and minds, the words simply bounce off our outer ears and land on the floor. And they can't penetrate our minds if we are thinking about the lunch we must prepare, the shopping we must do, or the emails, tweets and Facebook posts we must respond to. How often we sit down to read the Bible and pray, only to have thoughts of the tasks on our to-do lists or the immediate needs of family drown out the communication between us and God. In those moments, a choice presents itself: we can yield to the need to get busy with the day, or resist that pull and apply ourselves to the one needful thing—hearing God's voice through his Word and responding to him in prayer. This is one of those many choices that become easier each time we make it.

Martha's choice, although it was certainly proper to provide for the Lord Jesus and the others, was less than the best choice because it closed her ears to truth, and the result of that choice was a heart that became resentful and angry toward her sister and accusatory and demanding toward Jesus. Her attitude became unlovely and unloving because of her choice. Mary's choice was to be at his feet where she found peace, joy and purity. To choose to be anywhere else today is to give in to the allure of a world that seeks to conform us to its image— silly, self-absorbed, sexually obsessed, and materialistic.

Our lives are so full of the frivolous and unnecessary, all the things that stifle faith and devotion to God. Mary's choice of the better was the result of the astonishing, breathtaking faith developed in her over years of focusing on Jesus and seeing him through the eyes of discernment. Oh, if we only had that kind of faith and commitment, the kind that drives us to choose the one thing we truly need—to see the beauty of the Lord like David:

'One thing I have desired of the LORD,
That will I seek:
That I may dwell in the house of the LORD
All the days of my life,
To behold the beauty of the LORD,
And to inquire in His temple'
(Psalm 27:4).

# 5

# Coming to him:
# the education of Martha

We now fast-forward several months to the event outlined in John 11:1–44. It is winter, Jesus' last winter on the earth. The cross awaits him in the spring of that year. He travels to Perea, northeast of Jerusalem and continues healing the afflicted and teaching his disciples through parables. While staying in Betharaba, the scene of his baptism (John 10:40), he receives a message from Martha and Mary that their brother is desperately ill. It is fitting that they would send for Jesus; they were close friends and their relationship was characterized by love and care. Of course they believed that he had power to heal Lazarus (John 11:21), as they had seen and heard of his many healing miracles in the past. Whether or not they believed Jesus would heal their brother, they were eager for him to know that the one he loved was on the brink of death. The sisters had no doubt he would desire to see his beloved friend before it was too late.

They dispatched a messenger to where Jesus was staying, some twenty miles away from Bethany, a one-day's journey on foot. We don't know how they knew of his location. Perhaps they received regular updates on his activities; in any case, news of his miracle healings traveled quickly through the area. When Lazarus became dangerously ill, they knew it was time to send for the one who loved him. No doubt they expected him to hurry to Lazarus's bedside and arrive the following day. But four days went by with no word from Jesus, and while they were waiting for him, Lazarus died. We can only imagine the grief that overwhelmed the sisters, along with the questions that must have troubled them: *Where was Jesus? Why didn't he come?*

How often we ask the same questions when God fails to arrive on the scene of our misfortunes! *Where is he? Doesn't he know? Doesn't he care?* Of course Jesus knows and of course he cares. But sometimes he has a higher purpose for the troubles he allows to afflict us. This is the mystery of the divine will—sometimes he allows us to understand why he does things; sometimes he doesn't. All we really need to know is that 'his way is perfect' (Psalm 18:30). In this case, he not only knew of Lazarus's death; he also knew it was foreordained 'for the glory of God, that the Son of God may be glorified through it' (John 11:4). So that there would be no doubt in anyone's mind when the miracle of resurrection took place, Jesus waited two days before leaving. Including the day for the messenger to reach him, plus the day for Jesus to travel to Bethany, by the time he arrived, four days had passed. Lazarus was well and truly dead.

Those four days passed in the Jewish custom of mourning. Lazarus was laid in a tomb cut into a hillside, a stone was rolled across the entrance to the tomb, and Mary and Martha returned to their home to perform the mourning rituals. Their home was filled with friends who came to comfort them, along with many Jews from Jerusalem. Finally they received word that Jesus was coming. Martha responded immediately by leaving the house and going to meet him on the road. Rushing up to him, her first words were, 'Lord, if You had been here, my brother would not have died' (John 11:21). We can almost hear the additional unspoken question that must have been nagging at her for four days. *So why weren't you here?!* She knew he was only a day's journey away. Why had he waited so long? He had healed so many complete strangers. Why had he not been here to heal her brother? What possible reason could he have for the delay? She was about to find out and receive from him truths that would change her life forever.

## The education of Martha

Martha was standing before the Great Teacher, the One whose wisdom far exceeds that of mortals. He knew all that had happened in the past four days. He had even told the disciples that his plan was to go to Bethany to wake Lazarus from the sleep of death (John 11:11–16), although they didn't comprehend his meaning. Ever the patient and loving Lord, he imparted the same truth to Martha and she, like the disciples, didn't quite grasp it. Like so many of us, Martha was fixed on what Jesus could do for her and for her brother. Before this short, but life-changing lesson was over, she would have a completely different way of thinking, one that lined up more with that of Mary.

She added another statement to her opening accusation, perhaps as a way to soften it. 'But even now I know that whatever You ask of God, God will give You' (John 11:22). It was as though she was saying, *You missed your opportunity, but you have the means to make amends.* Jesus had failed to do what she expected of him, but even now he can *do something* to make it alright. Whether she had the actual resurrection of Lazarus in mind is uncertain, but whatever she wanted him to ask of God, there was some course of action she wanted him to take. Like so many competent, efficient people, she was fixated on what could be done. That type of person approaches every problem in the same way: *We need to do something!* It must have been simply maddening for her to see Jesus standing there calmly when he could have been acting to remedy the situation.

Jesus then assured her that her brother would rise again. Martha knew all about the resurrection of the dead in the last days. She believed there would be a resurrection of the dead at the end of the world, and that her brother would rise at that general resurrection. She had faith in what would come to pass eventually, but her concern was for the here and now. Perhaps she was thinking, *but what about now? Aren't you going to do something?* No doubt Martha received great consolation from her faith in the final resurrection and from her faith in Jesus' ability to heal the sick. Hadn't she heard of his many miracles? She just wished he could do one of those miracles now. *Ask the Father. He'll do what you ask. I know my brother will rise eventually, but what about now? Please DO something.* What Jesus was about to teach her is the truth that calms the heart of even the most action-oriented person. He began by telling her not what he could do or would do, but *who he is:* 'I am the resurrection and the life. He who believes in Me, though he may die, he shall live.'

Some people are just 'wired' to take action, while others are more thoughtful and observant. Martha reminds us of Peter, another man of action, whose first response to most situations was to *do something.* On the Mount of the Transfiguration, Peter saw Jesus, transformed into his true glory, speaking with Moses and Elijah. Peter's response was to initiate a building project—the erecting of three tabernacles. His natural response to something he couldn't quite understand was to get busy and do something, anything. We can almost hear him babbling away about his plan, only to be interrupted by a voice from heaven: 'While he was still speaking, behold, a bright cloud overshadowed them; and suddenly a voice came out of the cloud, saying, "This is My beloved Son, in whom I am well pleased. Hear Him!"' (Matthew 17:5). In other words, 'Stop talking and listen!' Peter's response? Silence. He and the other two disciples fell on their faces in awe and reverent fear (v. 6). Peter stopped talking and started worshiping because he had received the understanding that Jesus was the Son of God.

Here was the same lesson Martha learned on the road to Bethany, the same lesson we must learn if our lives have any hope of being characterized by peace, joy and confidence. It's not about what Jesus can or should do for us, nor is it about what we can do for him. It's about *who he is*. When Jesus told Martha, 'I am the resurrection and the life,' he was making one of the 'I AM' statements about himself found in John's Gospel. Each one reveals truth about who he is: 'I AM the Bread of life' (6:35,41,48,51); 'I AM the Light of the world' (8:12); 'I AM the Door of the sheep' (10:7,9); 'I AM the Good Shepherd' (10:11,14); 'I AM the Way, the Truth and the Life' (14:6); 'I AM the true Vine' (15:1,5). By using the phrase 'I AM', Jesus was declaring his deity, referring back to the 'I AM' of the Old Testament (Exodus 3:6). Jesus was assuring Martha that he was God in flesh, the life-changing truth that gives proper perspective to all of life's circumstances. God himself was standing before her, speaking to her, loving her. When she comprehended this amazing reality, her questions ceased and she affirmed her faith in who he was, not in what he would do.

When we come at last to understand who Jesus is, not just what he can do for us, we begin to see through the fog of the natural flesh that is always 'do-oriented.' Similarly, we must see ourselves in the light of who we are in Christ, not simply what we can accomplish for him. This is the knowledge that brings peace and joy. At this point, Martha becomes more like her sister—quiet, confident, and at peace. When she was able to say, 'I believe that You are the Christ, the Son of God, who is to come into the world' (v. 27), her faith had grown to the level of Mary's. Nothing gives a woman peace and confidence like the sure knowledge of her God, his nature and attributes, especially his sovereignty— his absolute control over all of life's circumstances, and his perfect plans and purposes. Somewhere along the line, Mary had already come to that knowledge and it produced in her the peace that 'passes all understanding' (Philippians 4:7). It showed every time Mary appears, in the way she chooses the truly essential over the mundane, in the way she responds to harsh criticism, and in the way she exhibits uncanny understanding of Jesus' mission on earth that others couldn't grasp. This same peace and confidence is available to all of us through the intimate knowledge of our God, 'as His divine power has given to us all things that pertain to life and godliness, *through the knowledge of Him* who called us by glory and virtue' (2 Peter 1:3, emphasis added).

## Martha's transformation

For many women, our view of God is based on what he does or doesn't do in our lives. The events of our lives, then, become the determiner of our feelings toward God. If he does what we feel is the 'loving' thing to do, then we deem him to be a loving God. If he provides employment, we proclaim his faithfulness as a provider. If wrongs committed against us are righted (and of course in our own timing), we proclaim his justice. If he answers our heartfelt prayers, we are confident of his mercy and grace. But what happens when a child is struck down by a terminal illness, when unemployment impoverishes the family, when we suffer injustice at the hands of those we thought were one in Christ with us, or when our prayers seem to go unanswered? Do we still, through these circumstances, proclaim God's love, justice, mercy and grace? We do if we truly know him, apart from life's circumstances. But when we allow the temporal to influence our perspective on the eternal, instead of the other way round, our view of God becomes distorted and our faith is shaken.

One of the most disturbing trends in modern Christianity is the tendency to minimize the most stunning, earth-shattering event in all of human history—the Incarnation. God, the Creator of heaven and earth, the omnipotent, transcendent, holy Lord of all, condescended to come to earth as a man, submit himself to evil men, die on the cross for our sins, make us quite literally 'partakers of the divine nature' (2 Peter 1:4), and enable us to spend eternity in heavenly bliss. And all of this was done, not because we deserved this inestimable privilege or in any way earned it, but simply because God determined to do it for his own glory and his name's sake. We have said it so many times and affirmed its truth so often that we lose sight of the incredible nature of the act itself. *Yes, Lord, I believe you died to save me. I accept Jesus as my Savior. Now what are you going to DO for me?* As though what he has already accomplished isn't enough! As though the glory of the

Incarnation was merely a starting point from which more and better blessings must flow, and if those blessings are slow in coming, or they in some way fail to meet our expectations, the impact and importance of the Incarnation itself is diminished.

This was the point of Martha's educational experience. She quite literally saw the Light, standing before her, proclaiming his deity. Who but God himself could make the statement, 'I am the resurrection and the life'? There was nothing more to say, nothing left for him to do for Martha to apprehend this amazing reality. All that was left for Martha to say was, 'Yes, Lord, I believe that You are the Christ, the Son of God, who is to come into the world.' So it is with us. Each of us must come face to face with the reality of who Jesus is, not of what he may or will or should do for us. If he did absolutely nothing except save us and preserve us for heaven, that one incredible blessing should be more than sufficient to produce in us unending joy and peace. The fact that he does so much more is testimony of his limitless grace and benevolence toward the undeserving.

The next time we see Martha, she is still serving, but this time in peace and quietude (Matthew 26:6; John 12:2). The amazing thing about that final incident is that she is serving in the house of someone else, Simon the leper, as though she were a hired domestic. Martha was a homeowner and a woman of some wealth, as witnessed by her ability to provide for the large number of people Jesus brought with him whenever he came to Bethany. The number of mourners and Jews attending Lazarus's funeral also speaks to her place in the community. The very expensive perfume that Mary owned also indicated that these three siblings were well-off, the kind of people who hired servants for themselves. For Martha to take the place of a lowly servant in the house of another shows that she had attained the true humility that comes from a life-altering encounter with God in flesh.

The Lord Jesus would teach that same humility to the disciples in the days to come, humbling himself to the level of the lowest servant and washing their feet (John 13:5). Martha's encounter with Jesus on the road produced in her true humility and it increased her faith, a faith which had been defective due to a lack of appreciation of the person of Christ. Like Martha, we must set our hearts to 'grow in the grace and knowledge of our Lord and Savior Jesus Christ' (2 Peter 3:18). We can attain neither humility nor true peace without that knowledge.

## Mary comes to Jesus

Immediately after her affirmation of the person of Christ, Martha went home to call her sister, saying, 'The Teacher has come and is calling for you' (John 11:28). There was a time when Martha would have called Mary away from Jesus; now she calls her sister to him. We don't know why Mary remained in the house at first. Whatever the reason, she ran to Him in obedience when called. Perhaps the reason Martha went out without telling Mary and when she came back, told her 'secretly' about Jesus is that the Jewish custom was for mourners not to leave their homes the first week after the burial.

If that is the case, it is further proof that Mary had no problem defying customs where the presence of Jesus was concerned. Just as in the other two incidents with Mary and Jesus, she showed again her willingness to break cultural customs for love of him.

Upon finding Jesus on the road, Mary makes her only statement—the one and only thing Mary is ever recorded as saying in all of Scripture. She says exactly what Martha had said to him, 'Lord, if You had been here, my brother would not have died' (v. 32). Unlike Martha, however, she fell at his feet while saying it. This was an affirmation, not an accusation, nor was it followed by a request for him to do anything. Hers was a proclamation of deity and an act of worship.

Even so, Mary still sorrowed and wept over the death of a beloved brother. Lazarus was most likely the youngest of the three siblings. The fact that he was still living at home with his sisters and there is no mention of their parents leads us to wonder if Mary could have been more like a surrogate mother to him than a sister. While Martha was the head of the household, Mary seems to have been its heart. She may have raised her brother from a very young child, perhaps even from his infancy. Some commentators have suggested that her weeping at the feet of Jesus was an indication of her faltering faith, but nothing in any of the Bible passages about Mary affirms that supposition or even hints at it. Her adored little brother had just died. Of course she was weeping!

How typical is this of the two aspects of the life we endure on this planet! We rejoice in the nature of Christ and enjoy his love and tender care for us, but there will always be sorrow and weeping here. Job 5:7 reminds us that man is born to trouble as surely as the sparks fly upward, but we are also assured that 'weeping may endure for a night, But joy comes in the morning' (Psalm 30:5). All sorrow here is mitigated by the joy that is before us, and we do not sorrow as those who have no hope (1 Thessalonians 4:13). Weeping at the terrible events of life does not signify a lack of faith. Rather, it points to our humanness and the fallen world we live in.

Unlike Martha, Mary requires no lesson concerning the deity of Christ in this incident. She already knows exactly who he is. Just a few short months later, she will again fall before him and revere him in the way only God himself merits our reverence. She will worship him because he deserves her worship, with no thought for what she can get out of it. Her faith in him is monumental, unshakeable, and transcendent, born of a deep, intimate knowledge of him, and it is that great faith which brings about his commendation of her.

# 6

# What she has done: Mary's good work

We come now to the most amazing part of Mary's mystery story, her final earthly encounter with Jesus and the good work she performed that elicited his praise. So familiar is this incident that we can easily miss the true meaning of her act and the heart condition that prompted it. Much has been written and much speculation has been offered as to what exactly Jesus was commending Mary for. In order to solve the mystery, we have to eliminate the things he was not referring to.

There are various theories on what was extraordinary about Mary's actions on this occasion. Some believe it was the cost of the perfume, which has been estimated at a year's wages. 'Nard' or 'spikenard' was brought from the East Indies sealed in alabaster jars or vials. So precious and expensive was this perfumed oil that it was used only a tiny bit at a time to make it last many years. Pouring it out all at once produced a fragrance so powerful that it filled the house (John 12:3) and drew the attention of everyone at the table. Was Jesus praising Mary for pouring out a year's wages worth of this substance on him at one time? Was it the expense that impressed Jesus? More to the point, is Jesus *ever* impressed by the use of money in his cause? Did he ever praise anyone for giving large sums of money? Biblically speaking, the answer to these questions has to be 'no.' We have only to look at the many incidents in his life and at the things he said about money to know that Jesus placed no value whatsoever on the world's wealth, and clearly Mary did the same. In fact, it was Judas, the keeper of the purse, the thief and traitor who betrayed the Lord to the Pharisees for thirty pieces of silver, who was concerned about the cost of the nard, not Jesus. So it cannot be the monetary value of the oil she poured over him that rendered her work worthy of his praise.

Perhaps it was her act of worship and adoration that prompted his praise of her good work. No doubt Jesus valued worship because he alone was worthy of it. But Mary was not the only one who worshiped the Lord while he was on earth. Many did the same, but none of them received a commendation like hers, much less a promise that their act of worship would be told throughout the ages as a memorial to them. The leper in Luke 5, the ruler in Matthew 9 did the same, the demon-possessed man in Mark 5, the blind man in John 9—all worshiped Jesus, but none of them received a tribute comparable to that given to Mary.

It has also been suggested that it was Mary's unashamed use of her hair to wipe Jesus' feet that was the source of his commendation. There is no doubt that a woman in that culture who uncovered her head and 'let down her hair' was making a very personal and intimate statement about the one she was ministering to. But her doing so was not unique. The woman in Luke 7:37–38 also came with oil to anoint Jesus, using both her hair and her tears to wash and wipe his feet as an act of loving worship. While Jesus commended her for her love and her faith and assured her that her sins were forgiven, he never said that her act would be told as a memorial to her down through the ages.

## Mary's good work

Jesus' commendation of Mary was a unique act of praise for a unique work. To solve the mystery and understand the singular nature of Mary's good work, we look at Jesus' words as described by Matthew and Mark. In both Gospels, Jesus' commendation was immediately preceded by a reference to her preparing him for burial:

'For in pouring this fragrant oil on My body, *she did it for My burial.* Assuredly, I say to you, wherever this gospel is preached in the whole world, what this woman has done will also be told as a memorial to her' (Matthew 26:12–13, italics added).

'She has done what she could. *She has come beforehand to anoint My body for burial.* Assuredly, I say to you, wherever this gospel is preached in the whole world, what this

woman has done will also be told as a memorial to her"
(Mark 14:8–9, italics added).

Here, then, is the key to the memorial to Mary and to
solving the mystery of her good work: *she came to anoint
Jesus for his burial.* This astonishing act was unparalleled
in all of Scripture. She alone among all those recorded
in the Bible knew that his death and burial were only
days away. She alone believed him when he said he 'must
suffer many things, and be rejected by the elders and
chief priests and scribes, and be killed, and after three
days rise again' (Mark 8:31). And that knowledge was
born out of her unique faith—faith in who Jesus was
and what he came to accomplish for her and for all who
would ever believe in him down through the ages.

Some have suggested that Jesus would never entrust
such astounding truths as these—the incarnation,
crucifixion, resurrection and substitutionary atonement
—to a mere woman. But once again, there is biblical
evidence to disprove this suggestion. It was to a woman
that Jesus revealed for the very first time his identity as
the Messiah, the Christ who was prophesied to come into
the world (John 4:5–26). And it was not just any woman
who received this astounding revelation from Jesus, but a
Samaritan woman, a lowly and despised adulteress. Prior
to this incident, it is never recorded that Jesus had made
so clear a revelation of himself to anyone. If he would
reveal such amazing truth about his identity to a sinful
Samaritan woman, can we doubt that he would reveal
his death and resurrection to Mary, a beloved friend and
godly woman? But men have always wondered at Jesus'

choice to disclose truth to women. Just as the disciples
'marveled that He talked with [Samaritan] woman' (v.
27), there are those who insist that Mary anointed Jesus
for burial, unaware of the meaning and significance of
her act.

We don't know how Mary came by this unique
knowledge born of faith or why Jesus chose to reveal to
her mind that which others could not grasp. This, too,
is a mystery. Many Bible commentators, some of whom
I admire greatly, have stated that Mary did not know
what she was actually doing in anointing Jesus at that
moment. Some have also suggested that she was like
the high priest Caiaphas who prophesied unknowingly
that Jesus was to die for the sins of the nation (John
11:49–51). But Caiaphas was an evil man, the head of the
faction whose intent was to destroy Jesus. Yet, as wicked
as he was, and as little as he intended it, God so ordered
it that he delivered the truth respecting the atonement.
Mary, on the other hand, had committed her life to
Jesus. Her only desire was to know him, be near him and
minister to him. Her knowledge of his fate was gained
from listening to him describe it and believing what he
said.

To equate Mary's act of faith with the statement of an
unbeliever whose words, completely unknown to him,
turned out to be prophetic, is to do Mary a terrible
disservice. Not only that, but why would Jesus commend
her in such glowing terms for her act when she had no
idea what she was doing? We simply can't ignore Jesus'
own words: 'She has kept this for the day of my burial.'
Her anointing him, at that particular time and in that

particular way, can only mean she was fully aware of the significance of her act. Caiaphas's prophecy is actually described in Scripture as not having been uttered out of his own 'accord' (ESV), 'initiative' (ISV) and 'authority' (NKJV). Clearly, he spoke 'not of himself' (KJV). There is no such statement about the source of Mary's knowledge; there is not a shred of evidence from the text to support the claim that Mary's act was done unknowingly. In fact, the text and the words of Jesus himself give ample evidence to the exact opposite.

Jesus said 'she has kept this [ointment] for the day of My burial' (John 12:7). The Greek word translated 'kept' means 'to hold fast, to guard, to reserve for some future event.' The same word is used in John 2, where the master of the feast is said to have *reserved* the good wine until the guests had had their fill. The same Greek word appears twice in Acts 25:21, referring to Paul: 'But when Paul appealed to be *reserved* for the decision of Augustus, I commanded him to be *kept* till I could send him to Caesar." So clearly Mary had saved, kept, and reserved the ointment until it would be needed to anoint Jesus for burial. If she did not know his burial was at hand, why would she have come at that exact moment, when she had saved the ointment, possibly for years?

Further, when Jesus said she had kept it for the 'day' of his burial, he did not mean that he would be buried that very day. The word translated 'day' can mean 24 hours, or any part of a day, or a period of time, indicated by the context. Clearly what is meant here is a period of time. If it was meant as the literal burial day, then Mary was pouring the ointment on him at the wrong time. The 'day' of his burial was meant as the general time period of his burial, which was still two days away, just as the 'day of the Lord' (John 8:56) and the 'day of salvation' (2 Corinthians 6:2) refer to general periods of time. But this was the last time Mary would have a chance to anoint him 'beforehand' for his burial. She couldn't stop him from going to the cross, she couldn't stop his death, but she 'did what she could'—she prepared him for his burial.

It's also amazing to see Mary's act in the light of the gospel itself. It is significant that Jesus said Mary would be memorialized 'wherever this gospel is preached in the whole world'. That simple, yet profound, statement connects Mary to the gospel forever. It makes her an advocate for the ultimate plan for the salvation of mankind. By preparing Jesus for the death and burial she knew was imminent, she showed that she not only understood the plan, but that she *submitted* to it in faith. She displayed the same kind of godly submission to the will of God that Jesus showed, the same submissiveness that all women of faith should display, even in the face of unpleasant circumstances. Mary understood that as horrible as crucifixion, death and burial of her beloved Lord was, the good news is that it was to be followed by resurrection, the singular most important act in human history and the one that would pave the way to eternal life for all of us. Unlike Peter, whose response to the plan was 'Never, Lord … This shall never happen to you!' (Matthew 16:22), Mary's response was *Yes, Lord, thy will be done.* By lining herself up with the will of God, she actively and consciously united herself for centuries to come with the gospel of salvation.

This was Mary's good work—an act of love and worship knowingly done in preparation for the single most important event in all of human history. Jesus' commendation was not just for Mary's love and adoration, but mostly for her great faith. She *believed* him when he revealed the plan of salvation, she took to heart this revelation, she submitted herself to it heart and soul, and she acted upon it at the appropriate moment. Like all acts of great faith, it was based on an intimate knowledge of the nature and character of God and the unshakeable belief that when he says something, he means it. There was no doubt in her mind as to Jesus' deity and what he came to accomplish. That insight and faith in him had prompted her to sit at his feet hearing his words and caused her to run to him when called and fall at his feet in worship of his deity, even though her heart was breaking at the loss of her brother. Mary's spiritual understanding and her deep faith, manifested in her final act of service to him, was the basis of Jesus' commendation of her.

Although good works are spoken of frequently in the Epistles, the phrase 'good works' only appears two other times in the Gospels, both spoken by Jesus himself. Good works come from the Father (John 10:32) and good works are those that glorify God (Matthew 5:16). Mary's act of faith fulfilled both requirements. Works done out of faith will always be from God because faith itself is a gift of God (Ephesians 2:8–9), and truly good works always have God's glory as their chief end. Works not born of faith and those which are done to bring honor and glory to the one performing them will never be deemed 'good' in the eyes of God. Mary's anointing of Jesus was prompted by her faith in who Jesus was—God in flesh—and that faith could only have come from him. In preparing him for burial, her work also glorified the Father, whose perfect plan of redemption was about to unfold.

## Examining our work

As Christian women, we all want to please the Lord who paid for our sin on the cross, who sanctifies us throughout our lives, and who preserves us for heaven. We want to be busy in his service. We want to please him with our sacrifices on his behalf. We want to tell others about him and let our light shine forth so they see him in us. That's what keeps us busy in acts of service. But Martha was certainly busy in serving, yet her service was less than the best. So often much of what we attempt for God falls into the Martha category. Why?

For one thing, her original service for the Lord had the wrong motive and made it, therefore, of no eternal value. Our works for God, done with the wrong motive or attitude, will never be commended by him. Many will come to Jesus in the last days, proclaiming their many deeds done in his name. They will say, 'Lord, did we not ...?' But he will say, 'I never knew you.' Jesus knows whose works are done for his glory and whose are done for their own sake. Many will claim to know Jesus and be known by him, only to be cast away from him forever. Their conversions will be determined to be false conversions, their works done only for their own glory. Even the works of true believers will be tried and tested by fire. Those who build worthless works, called 'wood, hay and stubble' in 1 Cor. 3:12, on the foundation that is Christ will find them burned up, while those who build 'gold, silver and precious stones' upon him will see their works shine through all eternity.

The difference between good works and worthless works is a matter of motive. I have known so many women who wore themselves out working in churches for the wrong motive. They worked in the nursery or children's Sunday school classes because no one else was willing to do it, not because their hearts burned with a passion for little ones to know Jesus. Some sang, played instruments, or performed in some way because they loved the attention and applause, not because their hearts were filled with love and gratitude to God that poured out in their music. Others taught classes and Bible studies because they loved the preeminence and control over others, or the social interaction, not because their desire was to see others 'grow in grace, and in the knowledge of our Lord and Savior Jesus Christ' (2 Peter 3:18).

We should all be examining our works to see if they are done for the eyes and good opinions of others, or to elevate ourselves, or if they are done out of a heart for God, a passion to see him glorified and obeyed, and a desire to further his kingdom. Acts 8 tells of a man named Simon who saw many signs and wonders done by the apostles, and desired the same power that was evident in them. He desired it so much as to offer money to them, as though money could purchase such a gift. But Peter saw his motive, and he discerned that Simon's heart was not right in the sight of God (v. 21). None of our works, no matter how glorious they may seem to us and to others, will be commended by God unless their motive is pure. No work of service in our churches, no sacrifice of time or money, no amount of tearful, emotional outpourings of praise, will receive the Lord's commendation unless it comes from a heart tuned in to his plans and purposes, not our own.

The only way to be sure our hearts and motives are right before God is to do what Mary did—sit at his feet, learn of him, hear his words, ponder them, and put them into practice. Perhaps even more important is to submit willingly to his words, as Mary did. When we say *Yes, Lord, your will be done,* we express our trust in him, affirming our faith and our absolute conviction that whatever he purposes is perfect, holy, and righteous. This kind of faith is the basis for true love and devotion and comes only from knowledge of him through his Word (2 Timothy 3:16–17). It goes without saying that we can't trust or love someone we don't know. So knowing God becomes the most crucial use of our time, and it is the only way to be sure our works mirror those of Mary.

# 7

# Mary's insight: knowing what others missed

Mary showed an uncanny understanding of Jesus' destiny; the disciples displayed just the opposite. By taking a close look at their reactions to Jesus' explicit declaration of the fate that awaited him in Jerusalem, we can see clearly the kinds of things in our own lives that prevent us from understanding spiritual truth. Hopefully, we can avoid the emotional devastation that can result when God's plans don't line up with our own.

Three times the twelve disciples heard Jesus' revelation about his future death, burial and resurrection. Peter, James and John heard it four times (Luke 9:28–31). And those are just the times recorded in Scripture. He could have discussed it with them many more times. Matthew and Mark record the first incident in some detail. 'From that time on, Jesus began to explain to his disciples that he must go to Jerusalem and suffer many things at the hands of the elders, chief priests and teachers of the law, and that he must be killed and on the third day be raised to life' (Matthew 16:21). Peter's response to this disturbing news was to take Jesus aside and rebuke him. 'Never, Lord!' he said. 'This shall never happen to you!' (v. 22) No doubt Peter spoke out of a sense of devotion to his Lord, but he was unknowingly a tool of Satan. Jesus responded in a way that must have shocked and hurt Peter: 'Get behind Me, Satan! You are an offense to Me, for you are not mindful of the things of God, but the things of men' (v. 23). That must have been a terrible jolt to Peter, one that stunned him into silence.

Peter's offense, according to Jesus, was in having the 'things of men' in mind, rather than the things of God. Peter's priorities were typical of the carnal world: setting up an earthly kingdom, defeating the Romans, and ruling with Jesus in Jerusalem. The things of God involved obedience, sacrifice, and the salvation of mankind. Of course Satan would be opposed to that! His plan was the destruction of the souls of millions and he tried to use Peter to further that plan.

How often do we become tools of Satan, even when we believe we are doing that which pleases God? When we pursue our own plans for ourselves, our families and our churches, do those plans involve obedience and sacrifice? Or are they characterized by a desire to have our own way, control others, and be the center of attention? This is a hard thing to ponder for most women, but much harder is the thought that we might be in danger of hearing the same rebuke from Jesus that

Peter heard. We have only to look at Mary's humble acts to see that her priority was Jesus himself. Not only did she not dream of refuting or opposing his plan to submit himself for crucifixion and death, but she did what she could to facilitate it by preparing him for his burial. The 'things of men' were of no interest to her. She was completely tuned in to the things of God.

Jesus' second revelation about his future occurred only a short time afterward, as recorded by Matthew, Mark and Luke, each one adding different details regarding the response of the disciples. Matthew tells us they 'were filled with grief' (Matthew 17:23). Mark says they 'did not understand what he meant and were afraid to ask' (Mark 9:32). Luke adds that the understanding of what he meant 'was hidden from them, so that they did not grasp it' (Luke 9:45). Most likely, their grief was due to their not being able to understand what he was saying. They knew he was telling them something significant, and it pained them to realize that the One they loved was giving them some important information that they just couldn't grasp. Perhaps they were afraid to ask him about it for fear that he might respond with a harsh rebuke as he had with Peter.

That the meaning was hidden from them is another painful part of the story. It's not that God hid from them the understanding. Jesus even prefaced his revelation by saying, 'Let these words sink down in your ears' (Luke 9:44). In other words, *Listen! I'm going to tell you something important!* So clearly he was intending that they should get it. But their own prejudices, ambitions, and false notions blinded them to reality. Their preconceived ideas about Jesus, his plans for the future, and how they figured into those plans, were so set in their minds that anything not lining up with those ideas was automatically rejected. So it is with so many people today. The most straightforward truths of the Bible become unintelligible to many because they have embraced some belief or opinion beforehand which is erroneous, and which they are unwilling to abandon. When that happens, the false beliefs take on a life of their own and become the standard against which all truth is measured and through which Scripture is filtered. How often we do the same! We embrace the Bible when it reveals God's love and care for us, but when it tells us that care involves trials for our benefit, we resist.

What was missing from the disciples' reasoning was faith, the kind that Mary possessed, and the kind women so desperately need today. Jesus revealed his upcoming death and resurrection, but the disciples' small faith caused them to react with denials, sorrow, fear, and misunderstanding. Mary's enormous faith prompted her response. *He said he was going to die. I must prepare him for burial.* There was no denial on her part, no attempt to dissuade him from his path, no attempt to mix truth with her preconceived ideas about the Messiah. She accepted his words as truth and acted upon them accordingly.

## Ambition—the ultimate discernment killer

The third time Jesus tried to reveal his future to the disciples is the saddest of all. This occurred on his final trip to Jerusalem. Very soon the events Jesus had been describing would unfold. One last time he imparted the blueprint to his friends, and this time he added some gruesome details. He told them he would be 'mocked and flogged and crucified' (Matthew 20:19), and he would be turned over to the Gentiles who would 'spit on him' (Mark 10:32). One would think this graphic description of what awaited him would bring them to tears or at least stun them into silence. But instead, James and John immediately approached Jesus with a request to give them places of honor in the kingdom they were still convinced would soon be set up. They asked him to 'Grant us that we may sit, one on Your right hand and the other on Your left, in Your glory' (Mark 10:37). But was it Jesus' glory they were seeking? Or their own?

Jesus was to be glorified in the plan and purpose of God. He was to die on the cross for the sins of all those who would ever believe in him, be raised on the third day and provide eternal life for millions. James and John were seeking their own glory in the two most exalted positions in the earthly kingdom they still believed he had come to establish. So desirous were they of earthly honor that they even sent their mother to plead their case (Matthew 20:20). The result of this sad supplication was not only to further close their ears to truth, but it also caused the other disciples to become 'greatly displeased' with the wrong motives of the two brothers. No doubt anger and jealousy rose in them to see the two trying to curry favor and obtain positions from which to lord it over them. Ambition always closes our ears, keeps us from discerning truth, and separates us from others. God will never grant wisdom and discernment to those whose ambition gets the best of them. To verify that, we have only to look at the sad sagas of mega-pastors and ministry leaders who fell into sin because they were blinded by their desire for money, power and influence.

Mary's only ambition was to serve Jesus, know him, glorify him and worship him. She had no desire for anything more and certainly exhibited no desire for self-aggrandizement. Even Martha's 'service' for Jesus was self-serving at first. It wasn't until she came to grips with who he was—the Resurrection and the Life— that she realized her only true service was in saying, 'Yes, Lord, I believe.' That simple act of obedience and faith changed her heart and mind completely. But the disciples' ambition and self-seeking closed their ears and stunted their faith, which is why they scattered like terrified sheep the night Jesus was arrested. It wasn't until the Holy Spirit descended upon them in Acts 2 that they became the pillars of strength and confident faith who went on to impact the world for Christ. By then, of course, they no longer sought their own fame and praise; their only ambition was to glorify God. Mary's discernment, even before the giving of the Holy Spirit, foreshadowed the power that would fall upon all believers in the future, enabling all of us to exhibit supernatural faith and understanding through him.

## Discerning truth from falsehood

The disciples' inability to grasp truth from Jesus' lips

because of pride and ambition should be a warning to us all. Discernment, especially in spiritual matters, is stunted by anything that exalts the self. This was seen after Jesus revealed the future to the disciples the second time. Mark 9 records that they 'did not understand what he meant and were afraid to ask him about it' (v. 32), but instead of asking him or searching the Old Testament prophecies about the Messiah, they fell to arguing among themselves as to which of them was the greatest (v. 33–34). Of course Jesus knew what was in their hearts, just as he knew exactly what they were arguing about. But he gave them the chance to confess it on their own, which they never did. But rather than rebuke them, he taught them a valuable lesson about the greatness they were seeking. 'If anyone wants to be first, he must be the very last, and the servant of all' (v. 35).

Desire for the preeminence is a sure destroyer of discernment and wisdom. The Greek word for 'servant' in verse 35 is *diakonos,* from which we get 'deacon' or 'deaconess.' When those who hold the position of deacon or deaconess in a church see it as a place of authority rather than servanthood, all kinds of trouble erupts. I once sat in a meeting with a group of women and heard a deaconess claim she had been given authority by the church elders to rule the women. As my husband was an elder at the time, I knew she had been given no such authority. The elders understood that they had no authority to give, but that they themselves were servants and had put deacons and deaconesses in their positions to serve, not to rule. It should come as no surprise that the women's ministry in that church had a long history of strife and contentiousness. When pride and ambition create in us the desire to be great and to rule over others, wisdom and discernment, which are gifts of God through his Spirit, are withheld. 'God resists the proud, but gives grace to the humble' (1 Pet. 5:5).

Mary's lack of pride and ambition were evident in the position she always took when in Jesus' presence—at his feet. It was also displayed both times she was unfairly rebuked, first by Martha and then by the disciples. Both times, she did not respond. She did not defend herself or make excuses for her actions. Humility never leaps to its own defense, letting others do the defending instead. We can only imagine how gratifying it was for her to hear the Lord Jesus himself come to her defense. Knowing what others could not grasp because pride and ambition had stopped their ears must have been a source of sadness to her as well as satisfaction. This too is evidence of her discernment. When we understand spiritual truths that others find mysterious because of pride or ambition, it should cause us to be as sad for them as we are delighted for ourselves.

This is not meant to be a condemnation of the disciples. Once they received the Holy Spirit at Pentecost, they went on to turn the world upside down with the gospel. Where they had not understood Jesus' destiny before, they preached the cross with passion afterward. Where once they had scattered in fear for their lives, they became pillars of strength of the early church and, all except John, eventually were martyred for their faithful proclamation of Jesus. They became the foundation of the Christian church, with Jesus as the cornerstone. The work of these twelve men—the Eleven plus Matthias who replaced Judas—continues today, two thousand years later. Only the power of God could accomplish such a transformation.

For his own purposes, God chose to give Mary a unique understanding, along with a discerning faith greater than that of anyone who came before her, even before the gift of the Holy Spirit at Pentecost. Discernment in spiritual matters is a gift of God, given in some measure to all believers. The Holy Spirit, who leads us into all truth (John 16:13), imparts and interprets spiritual truth to us. But what we do with that truth determines whether we will be given more truth and even greater ability to discern it. Jesus warned his disciples to 'take heed how you hear. For whoever has, to him more will be given; and whoever does not have, even what he seems to have will be taken from him' (Luke 8:18). So it is with us today. May we all be as discerning as Mary, taking the solid, spiritual knowledge of divine things we have been given, seeking greater revelations, and applying them to benefit ourselves, our families, our churches, and the world.

# 8

# Silence:
# the lost art

I've always been saddened by the statement 'women talk too much.' I'm saddened not because I think the statement is untrue, but precisely because I think it has a great deal of truth to it. The state of 'talking too much', as applied to women, is not always a matter of the number of words we speak or the amount of time we spend talking, but the content of those words and the use of that time. There have been great thinkers and theologians of the past who practically never stopped talking. Aristotle, Thomas Aquinas, C. H. Spurgeon and Abraham Lincoln come to mind as men who spoke and wrote volumes. I doubt anyone ever said to them, 'you talk too much.'

Women are talkers by nature. As noted before, studies have shown that little girls have better verbal skills than boys, speak earlier, talk more and excel in verbal communication. Of course there are exceptions to the rule, but generally girls express themselves verbally while boys do so physically. Verbal communication fulfills our need to express our emotional nature as well as our passion for detail. This is, sadly, the basis of an enormous amount of conflict in marriage. Wives, especially those who are home all day, are desperate to share every detail of their day with their husbands. What they talk about isn't nearly as important as the act of talking itself because by conversing, women connect and bond. Most men, quite frankly, aren't interested in mundane details and don't find them the least bit fascinating. Men are 'big picture' people; women are detail oriented. Men are often bewildered at how women can talk for hours about an event or conversation that took only thirty seconds to unfold and wasn't all that interesting in the first place.

The problem is not that women talk too much. The problem is that we say too little. Modern culture has given women numerous outlets to fulfill their need to communicate. Personal electronic devices enable us to keep up a constant stream of chatter every minute of the day. It used to be that we could only access others by telephone via a land line. Mobile phones now enable us to talk and text while we drive, stroll through the mall, walk the dog, shop for food, and eat in restaurants. But how many of those communications could be described as profound? Or even important? Very few. As one pundit described modern communication, 'never have so many said so much about so little.' Part of the mystery of Mary of Bethany is that she had very little to say.

Scripture records her uttering only one statement and yet she is the recipient of the highest level of praise and commendation from Jesus.

As women, the need to talk is directly related to the level of emotion we experience. So deeply do we feel things that we simply have to let it out verbally or we feel as though we will burst. The pressure that builds up from our emotions needs an outlet. Keeping all that emotion pent up inside us creates unbearable tension, and the way we relieve it is twofold: tears and talking. Just as we feel better after a good cry, we feel greatly relieved by pouring forth our emotions verbally. I once sat and listened to an emotionally distraught woman trying to weep and talk at the same time. To say she didn't make much sense is an understatement, but she certainly felt better for having unloaded all the emotional turmoil within her.

## Noisy and empty

Western culture is filled with noise. In the U.S. every public place comes with the obligatory musical background. Every store, mall, restaurant, airport, and office building has music piped in to bombard us with a continual stream of noise. One local outdoor mall has music coming from speakers hidden in the shrubbery, clashing with different music coming from each store one passes. The cacophony is overwhelming. Noise is so prevalent that we only notice when it is absent. Noise has become the norm; silence is the oddity. I remember landing in Zurich some time ago and walking off the airplane into the terminal where there was no music. I stopped suddenly and looked around, wondering if something was wrong. Had some national emergency occurred? No, it was just that, unlike Americans, the Swiss apparently didn't feel compelled to blast music into every public place. But I was so used to ubiquitous music in public places that silence was shocking to my senses.

In view of this constant barrage of noise—electronic, musical and conversational—is it any wonder that the disciplines of Bible study, prayer and especially meditation on the Word are in danger of being lost among Christians? Churches are rapidly adapting to the new norm, replacing Sunday school classes that once taught doctrine with interactive fellowship groups where everyone has their say. Electronic projections of Scripture and music lyrics on huge screens are also the rule, effectively doing away with pew Bibles and hymnals. Music often replaces preaching, or at least takes up an equal amount of time, Christmas cantatas and theatrical productions are offered in place of a Christmas sermon, and every missionary shows a video about their work in foreign countries. And that doesn't even include the millions of internet sites and blogs that purport to proclaim Christian truth.

Has all of this noise and technology produced a generation of strong, biblically sound Christians, armed with the life-changing truths of Scripture and making a difference in an increasingly ungodly world? If we're honest with ourselves, we have to say no. Never have Christians had so many opportunities to communicate while at the same time having so little understanding of the only things worth communicating. We make an enormous amount of noise, but our hearts and minds are too often devoid of real truth. As my mother used to say when I babbled on to no good end, 'empty barrels make the most noise.'

While my mother's adage might be amusing, it sadly reflects the state of the minds and hearts of so many of us today—empty. Western culture is self-obsessed and that self-obsession manifests itself in the endless barrage of words about the almighty self. This is the 'me/my' syndrome, this perpetual fascination with ourselves—what we think, how we feel, and what we have to say. The 'me/my' mania is everywhere and it has not escaped the notice of the marketing gurus. Internet addresses with the word 'my' in the name are prevalent. It seems that every company wants us to think they are in business for us alone. The goal is to make us feel good about ourselves and offer us something that even increases our already bloated self-esteem.

With all the words pouring forth from us, much of our conversations are still devoid of real substance. Mostly we think and talk about ourselves. In my book, *Freeing Tangled Hearts,* I made the point that women, when we are first in love, can't talk about anything other than the man we love because thoughts and feelings about him fill our minds and hearts.

'But if our minds are set on *us,* then *we* are all we talk about because we are all we're truly interested in. The culture of greed we live in encourages just this kind of thinking because when we are obsessing about ourselves, the inevitable result is discontent. And what do we do when we are discontented? We shop. We eat. We fill our lives with entertainment. Of course we find no cure for our discontentment in these things, which keeps us going back for more. This is the result of self-focus. The carnal self, the old person, is never satisfied. We have to stop feeding it.'

It would be one thing if all this obsession with self and the endless verbiage that accompanies it were producing a generation of Christians who are strong, filled with life-changing faith, and making a spiritual impact on the world. But that is not the case. Never has the Christian church been spiritually weaker and worldlier than it is today. What we need to understand is that the one needful thing is what Mary understood and which was reflected in her quiet grace and lack of self-focus. It's really not about us, despite what modern marketing is determined to convince us. It's about God. If only we could absorb that truth, the influence Christians could have on the world would be immense.

## Silence, understanding and a calm spirit

As Psalm 46:10 tells us, being still and knowing God go hand in hand. We will never have the kind of deep faith and quiet spirit that Mary had until we do what she did—sit at his feet, learn who he is, and submit to him. Remember that it wasn't until Martha was confronted with God in flesh that she stopped talking and started serving in peace and submission. When Jesus told her 'I am the Resurrection and the Life', her eyes were opened and she began to truly know him. At that point, she became still. Her heart, so flustered and distracted at first, began to settle into a calm and quiet understanding of the reality that it was God in flesh standing before her, loving her, caring for her and controlling all of life's circumstances, including death. What he would do or not do became irrelevant. *Who he is* became all-important. There was no longer a need to talk. She became the embodiment of Proverbs 17:27—'He who has knowledge spares his words, And a man [or woman] of understanding is of a calm spirit.'

Do you have a 'calm spirit'? If not, it's because you are not a woman of understanding who spares your words. That's not my assessment; it's that of the Holy Spirit through the writer of the proverb. According to this verse, the three concepts are inescapably linked together—knowledge (understanding), limited words, and a calm spirit. The word translated 'spares' means to restrain, reserve, or refrain. In other words, the woman of understanding and a quiet spirit is one who restrains her words and reserves her thoughts so that not everything that comes into her head comes out of her mouth. Not every idea, opinion or feeling needs to be expressed, nor should it be. In fact, we have to be careful how much we allow our mouths to run on. Another Proverb reminds us that 'in the multitude of words sin is not lacking, But he who restrains his lips is wise' (Proverbs 10:19). If our lives are characterized by a

'multitude of words,' we can be certain that sin will rear
its ugly head on a regular basis.

While Mary was lauded for her actions, not her words,
most women find themselves in the opposite situation—
bringing reproach upon themselves for the sins of their
tongues. Excess verbiage that is simply inane or silly is
one thing. The multitude of words that opens the door
for sin is another. If we who claim to know Jesus do not
restrain ourselves verbally, we have no reason to believe
our profession of faith is real. James warned of this very
thing: 'If anyone among you thinks he is religious, and
does not bridle his tongue but deceives his own heart,
this one's religion is useless' (James 1:26). No woman
wants to find out too late that her religion is useless.
Such will be the fate of those who deceive themselves
and who hear from Jesus the dreaded words, 'I never
knew you' (Matthew 7:23).

For women, who are often filled with anxieties and
negative emotions such as fear, doubt, and guilt, being
still means not being anxious, impatient, restless or
distracted like Martha. Instead, it means being quiet and
restful of spirit, delighting in the will of God, no matter
what that may be, and living in an assured expectation
that the divine will is perfect, holy, righteous and just.
Similarly, 'knowing' God means acknowledging that
he, and he alone, is God, a sovereign Being who does
whatsoever he pleases, 'according to His will in the army
of heaven And among the inhabitants of the earth. No
one can restrain His hand Or say to Him, "What have
You done?"' (Daniel 4:35).

Being still and knowing God means living in the

absolute assurance that he is unchangeable in his nature, purposes, and promises, that he is omnipotent, able to help and deliver us, and that he will never leave or forsake us. It means dwelling in the liberating confidence that he is omniscient, knows all our hardships and troubles, and how and where to hide us till the storm is over. It means having the deep and settled conviction that he is the all-wise God, and does all things after the counsel of his own will, that he makes all things work together for good, and that he is faithful to his word and promise. It is also knowing he will not allow us to be overwhelmed by troubles, but will, out of his great love, use such things to mature us and bring us to new heights of confidence, to our benefit and his glory.

This is what it means to be still and know God. It was what characterized the life of Mary of Bethany, whose great faith stilled her heart, limited her words and prompted her to the actions that would be told throughout the ages as a memorial to her.

# 9

# No self-defense:
# the mystery of humility

In view of the criticism leveled at her from those closest to her, Mary's silence is truly a mystery. We can only imagine how hurtful the words of her sister and Jesus' disciples must have been to her. The censure of complete strangers is one thing, but the unjust criticism from those we love and trust can be terribly upsetting. When others, especially those within the body of Christ, hurt and abuse us, the natural first response is to strike back; the second is to defend ourselves. That Mary did neither is truly remarkable and indicates that she must have had an extraordinary inner peace as well as complete confidence in her actions and in her motives.

Solving the mystery of Mary's responses to the attacks from those she loved and trusted can hopefully help us respond in a similar way when faced with injustice and injury inflicted on us by others. The first instance of unfair accusation came from her own sister. Martha, flustered and distracted about the serving, allowed her frustration to build up to the point that she went to Jesus to complain about Mary. She could have taken Mary aside quietly and asked her to help, but she chose instead to humiliate her sister publicly. How often this occurs today. How many of us have been the recipient of hurtful gossip and complaints against us? And those complaints are often about what we believe to be innocent or well-intentioned words or actions. Instead of going to one another quietly and gently explaining the problem, we so often emulate Martha, airing our grievances to others in order to appear the injured party and gain sympathy.

Mary could have responded angrily and defended herself. After all, she was being unfairly accused. She could have reminded Martha in front of everyone that Jesus' teaching was more important than the food. She could have called Martha's attitude into question. But this would only have worsened an already uncomfortable situation. So she wisely chose to be silent and allow Jesus to take up her defense. Psalm 7:10 may have come to Mary's mind: 'My defense is of God, Who saves the upright in heart.' She may have quickly examined her own heart and its motives and come to the conclusion that they were upright and therefore believed she could leave the defending to Jesus. True to Psalm 7:10, Jesus did come to her defense. When our hearts are right before him and the motivations for our words and actions are pure, we can leave the defense safely in his hands. He is, after all, the only one who can judge purely and justly all the circumstances and he alone 'knows the secrets of the heart' (Psalm 44:21).

Even more than the incident with Martha, Mary's final act of anointing Jesus for burial brought forth some of the most crushing criticism from those she most trusted. Their reactions as described in Mark 14:5 show the disciples at their worst. Interestingly, different English translations of that verse show us the different aspects of the Greek word for the disciples' response to her final act of worship. They 'criticized her sharply' (NKJV), 'scolded her' (ESV), 'murmured against her' (KJV), and 'rebuked her harshly' (NIV). Matthew adds that they were 'indignant.' In criticizing her sharply, the disciples accused Mary of doing something wrong. By scolding her, they belittled her and treated her like a naughty child. By murmuring against her, probably to one another, they banded together to make her the outsider. Rebuking her harshly gives the impression of trying to convince her to take a different course of action. All these different translations describe, in painful terms, their attitude toward her.

What was in their hearts that prompted such negativity? Perhaps they were upset that she had interrupted their meal or that she had done something they deemed inappropriate. After all, in order to wipe Jesus' feet, she loosened her hair, something an upright woman would never do in public. Whatever it was, their priorities were skewed, as witnessed by their saying that the perfume poured on Jesus was 'a waste' (Matthew 26:8; Mark 14:4). Again, we see human nature at its worst. The disciples not only criticized Mary to her face, but they murmured among themselves about her act. They also showed that they still didn't understand what awaited Jesus only days away. Worst of all, they accounted an act of worship toward him to be a waste, as though anything sacrificed for God in flesh could be considered a waste! In view of what he was to suffer for their (and our) sakes, it is stunning to see the callousness of their hearts. No doubt this sad episode came to mind after the crucifixion as they considered their betrayal and abandonment of him. We can only imagine the pain those memories must have caused them.

Just as Mary did not defend herself in the face of Martha's criticism, she showed remarkable restraint toward the disciples in spite of their unjust accusations against her. She could have rebuked them in kind, asking them why they didn't understand what Jesus had revealed about his upcoming death. She could have sought revenge by embarrassing them and reminding everyone of their failings. She could also have appealed to Jesus to defend her. But she did none of these things. She quietly and confidently went about the business of anointing Jesus for burial, content in the knowledge he had given her. No doubt she sensed that her understanding of spiritual truth was a gift from God and that he would, in his own perfect timing, grant to the disciples the same understanding. She was perfectly confident in his timetable. She knew there was no need to defend herself or pay back evil for evil.

Most of all, she relied on her rock solid faith, holding before her the shield of faith with which she could 'extinguish all the flaming arrows of the evil one' (Ephesians 6:16). It is obvious that Judas was the main instigator of the rebukes against Mary. Considering that Satan would enter into him and he would soon betray Jesus, her faith-shield was desperately needed to ward off the fiery darts directed at her by Satan through Judas. The question for us to consider today is whether we have faith similar to Mary's. Is our shield well-polished and held before us when we go into the battlefield of trying to live the Christian faith in a culture that hates us? Do we hold it before us with strong arms or does it slip down as we grow weary of the battle, particularly the one that is fought in our own churches? Do we leap to our own defense when our egos are wounded? Or are we confident enough in the rightness of our cause to leave the defending to our Rock and Redeemer?

## Mary was blessed

People today are no less cruel in their criticism of one another. Especially when we try to live righteous and upright lives, we can be the victims of the most unjust and unkind accusations. Others can murmur and gossip behind our backs. Or they confront us and question our motives. Sadly, this frequently comes from those who claim to be our brothers and sisters in Christ, and it is the cause of so much strife and discord in churches. But Jesus warned us of this very thing in the Sermon on the Mount. 'Blessed are those who are persecuted for righteousness' sake, For theirs is the kingdom of heaven. Blessed are you when they revile and persecute you, and say all kinds of evil against you falsely for My sake. Rejoice and be exceedingly glad, for great is your reward in heaven, for so they persecuted the prophets who were before you' (Matthew 5:10–12).

We expect those in the world to oppose us, but it is especially hurtful when it comes from within the body of Christ. Clearly, Mary was being reviled and persecuted for Jesus' sake and evil was spoken against her. Yet she showed no tendency toward retaliation. Perhaps she had been among the crowds who heard the Sermon on the Mount and took to heart Jesus' words about the persecuted being blessed, and maybe those words came back to her as she anointed Jesus. In any case, her silence indicated that she felt no need to defend herself. It also indicated humility, peace in her heart, and confidence in her chosen course of action.

When we are callously criticized and falsely accused, it should be cause for rejoicing. Jesus said that those who hate him would hate his followers as well. Paul adds, 'Yes, and all who desire to live godly in Christ Jesus will suffer persecution' (2 Timothy 3:12). In fact, if we are never mistreated for our faith, we have cause to wonder why. Fiery trials are to be expected, even when they come from within the church. But neither Jesus nor Paul ever recommended retaliation or self-defense. The psalmist reminds us to let God be our defender. 'But let all those rejoice who put their trust in You; Let them ever shout for joy, because You defend them; Let those also who love Your name Be joyful in You' (Psalm 5:11). Loving God's name will almost certainly bring suffering in some way. Like Mary, we simply must resist the temptation to strike back or get even.

Surely Mary must have been aware of Jesus' teaching on the Beatitudes, whether she was present during the Sermon on the Mount or heard them secondhand. 'Blessed are the poor in spirit, For theirs is the kingdom of heaven' (Matthew 5:3) may have also come back to her, reminding her that without the special revelation that Jesus had bestowed upon her, she would have been in the same condition as the disciples. She understood that poverty of spirit means we come to Jesus with nothing of worth to offer him, needing everything from him. We are spiritual beggars, standing with heads bowed like the tax collector in the Temple, unable to even look up and only capable of imploring, 'Lord, be merciful to me, a sinner' (Luke 18:13). Seeing others in that same light goes a long way to enabling us to forgive, just as Jesus forgave those who persecuted and murdered him. Hanging on the cross, he had only compassion for them, asking 'Father, forgive them, for they do not know what they do' (Luke 23:34).

If anyone had cause to retaliate against unjust accusations and harsh criticism, it was Jesus. Mary knew from what he had revealed about the coming days that he would experience unimaginable suffering at the hands of the Romans and the Jews. He would be betrayed by one of his own, arrested, beaten, humiliated, stripped naked, reviled, spit upon, then put to death in the cruelest way known at the time—crucifixion. Surely if Jesus could have such compassion on those who abused him so dreadfully, we who belong to him can find forgiveness and compassion in our own hearts, just as Mary did. Imitating Jesus' silence in the face of persecution, Mary aligned herself with her Lord. Perhaps she was reminded of lessons in Isaiah she had learned in the synagogue and took her cue from what was predicted there: 'He was oppressed and He was afflicted, Yet He opened not His mouth; He was led as a lamb to the slaughter, And as a sheep before its shearers is silent, So He opened not His mouth' (Isaiah 53:7). Like him, she chose silence over retaliation, revenge or self-defense. The basis for such a choice is humility.

## Blessed are the meek

We see in Mary and in the disciples two truths about humility. Mary's humility was evident in her words and her actions. The disciples' lack of humility was also evident in those two areas. Mary spoke little and acted humbly. Not so the disciples. Peter, for instance, was a great talker. He especially liked to talk about what he was going to do for Jesus. When Jesus told him that they would all be scattered like frightened sheep on the night of his arrest, Peter boldly asserted, 'Even if all fall away on account of you, I never will' (Matthew 26:33), and 'Lord, I am ready to go with You, both to prison and to death' (Luke 22:33), and 'I will lay down my life for Your sake' (John 13:37). Of course he failed to do any of these things, despite his brash confidence. Jesus knew Peter simply wasn't yet equipped to accomplish great things for the Lord. He also knew that Peter's failure would be the source of sorrow to him, but that he would return to his faith and through his failure he would be able to strengthen his brothers. What Peter lacked that Mary possessed was the wisdom that comes from humility. Proverbs 11:2 reminds us that 'When pride comes, then comes shame; But with the humble is wisdom.'

The disciples, too, evidenced a lack of humility when they argued among themselves about who would be greater in the kingdom. Out of their mouths came words of pride and boasting, motivated by the desire for the preeminent positions in the kingdom. Of course they were blinded to the truth that Jesus was trying to bestow upon them. They were shamed by their pride and the lack of wisdom that always accompanies arrogance. They sought honor from Jesus, which they believed they deserved, secure in the proud assessment of their own worth and their own abilities. But honor in the kingdom is never bestowed upon the proud. In fact, God will resist all our efforts when those efforts are motivated by pride. It is to the humble that he 'gives more grace.' That is why Scripture says: 'God opposes the proud but gives grace to the humble' (James 4:6). James goes on to encourage believers to 'Humble yourselves in the sight of the Lord, and He will lift you up' (James 4:10).

Mary sought nothing for herself. She only wanted to worship and love Jesus, to be near him, to listen to him, to know him, and to serve him. She was willing to humble herself at his feet, give him everything she had, and ask nothing in return. In her humility, she was like King Solomon, who when given the kingdom, admitted his deficiency: 'but I am a little child; I do not know how to go out or come in.' He asked only for a discerning heart in order to govern the people. God rewarded his humility with the greatest wisdom ever known. Moreover, God granted to him both riches and honor, even though he didn't ask for them (1 Kings 3:6–13).

In this age of bloated self-esteem and entitlement mentality, it is no wonder that true wisdom is sorely lacking. The spirit of this age is certainly pride and obsession with ourselves—how terrific we are and how much we deserve—the inevitable result of a too-high view of man and a too-low view of God. If we are ever to have the 'wisdom that comes from above', we must be like Mary and begin with a proper view of ourselves— lowly sinners in need of the grace of God. Then when we contemplate the amazing gift of eternal life, given freely to us when we neither earn it nor deserve it, humility is the natural result, as are the blessings that always accompany humility. 'But the wisdom that is from above is first pure, then peaceable, gentle, willing to yield, full of mercy and good fruits, without partiality and without hypocrisy. Now the fruit of righteousness is sown in peace by those who make peace' (James 3:17–18).

# 10

# Being a Mary in today's culture: is it even possible?

Mary's life seems so different from ours today. Hers was characterized by great faith and the peace that comes from it, while so many women today live lives of fear, insecurity, and a preoccupation with the mundane. As Christians who possess the gift of eternal life and the presence of God in our hearts, our focus should be more on the Lord who saved us and less on ourselves. But the current cultural mindset is to focus on ourselves, leaving God to become little more than a peripheral character. We should naturally be inclined to think more about an eternity in heaven that awaits us than about the 70 or 80 years we have here. But that, too, runs counter to the modern way of thinking. Perhaps being a Mary in today's culture is too far-fetched to be thinkable, but shouldn't Christians at least have that desire?

Mary's extraordinary actions were based on her extraordinary faith, a faith that is available to every one of us if we first understand that faith is a gift. We don't have that kind of faith within us when we are born and not even when we are born again. Ephesians 2:8–10 explains that saving faith is a gift from God, not something we earn. If it were, we would boast about it and take credit for it. God saves us by planting within us the faith to see our sinful condition and our need for a Savior. But the kind of faith Mary had goes beyond saving faith. It is the kind of faith that produces the wisdom to see behind the curtain of eternity into a world of the spiritual—God's world. It enables us to discern between the truth of God and the lies of the demonically controlled culture. But Mary's faith was also a gift of God, and if we are to have that kind of faith, we must ask for it.

Hebrews 12:2 describes Jesus as the 'author and finisher' of our faith. It comes from him as surely as a book comes from an author. He begins it, creates it, perfects it, and finishes it. Again, the key is in the asking. Jesus said if we ask, we will receive and if we seek, we will find. But so many of us don't ask or we ask for the wrong things, those which are not in his will because he knows they are not beneficial for us. But faith is one of those things we can be absolutely sure is God's will for us. So are discernment and wisdom. The problem with most people is that their desire for faith is not strong enough to keep them praying and asking for it. They don't see their small faith as the source of their turmoil. So the first order of business is to pray for that desire. As the desire for faith, for truth, for wisdom and discernment grows, we see that these too are all gifts from God. They become the desires of our hearts that God promised he would fulfill (Psalm 37:4).

Once we have the desire for faith, we also begin to desire to do the things Mary did that built and perfected her faith. First and foremost, she heard his word and she *believed* it. When he said he was going to Jerusalem to die and be raised again, she believed it. She didn't argue with him or try to dissuade him. She simply believed. The Bible is full of God's promises, and so often we say we believe them, but don't act accordingly. He says he works all things together for good to those who love him, but when things don't go our way, our first thought is often *God, why is this happening?* God promises that life on this earth is full of trouble and hardship, yet we still expect it to be ease and comfort. Although he says that the things of this world can never make us happy and fulfilled, we still pursue them. Why? *Because we don't really believe him.* Our faith is stunted by our own expectations of what the Christian life should be.

Mary believed Jesus was the Messiah, so naturally she was compelled to hear his every word. She believed in his deity, so of course the only appropriate place for her was at his feet. She believed him so completely that her response to his revelation of upcoming death was to anoint him for burial. What other reaction could she have in view of her absolute faith in him and his words? In everything she did, she exhibited an other-worldly faith, one that sees beyond the earthly into the eternal. Temporal circumstances did not skew her view of the spiritual realities behind them. The mystery of Mary is not that she received some kind of mystical messages from God as she sat at his feet. The mystery is the profound depth of her faith that gave her ears to hear his words. If we want that kind of faith, we must do what she did: hear his word and *believe* it.

## Believing God's promises

A Mary kind of faith has absolute trust in God's promises, but so often we expect the things God never promised. The disciples' limited faith caused them to believe that Jesus had come to do what they expected and desired of him, but this was due to a filtering of Old Testament prophecies about the Messiah through their own desires. They held tightly to the predictions of the One who would come to establish the throne of David forever (Isaiah 9:7), but ignored the prophecies that depicted the Messiah as 'despised and rejected by men, a Man of sorrows and acquainted with grief' (Isaiah 53:3). Like them, our weak faith tends to tune out the 'bad news' in the Bible and concentrate on those promises that line up with our expectations for ourselves.

God never promised health, wealth, perfect marriage, perfect children, or peace in this world. What he does promise is to supply all our needs (Philippians 4:19). Our problem is that we don't know what our needs really are and we don't have enough faith to allow him to determine our needs and fulfill them. Do we really understand that God has literally promised us 'all things' and that he has already given them to us? Does that mean he has promised all that would make life on this earth comfortable and pleasant? No, but he has promised that 'His divine power has given to us *all things that pertain to life and godliness,* through the knowledge of Him who called us by glory and virtue, by which have been given to us exceedingly great and precious promises, that through these you may be partakers of the divine nature, having escaped the corruption that is in the world through lust' (2 Peter 1:3–4). The 'all things' that God promised are the things that make our lives *godly,* not temporarily comfortable, affluent, and pain-free.

Another promise of God is in regard to temptations and trials, none of which can ever overcome us. God never promised that we would get to a certain point in our lives and be free of trials and temptations. In fact, he promised just the opposite. Jesus said 'in this life you will have trouble' (John 16:33). Job 14:1 says, 'Man born of woman is of few days and full of trouble.' Notice that it doesn't say 'unbelievers' or 'the ungodly'. It says man born of woman. And that means everyone. Life is full of trouble, even for those who belong to God through faith in Christ. We are to expect it. But God has assured us that no temptation or trial will overcome us (1 Corinthians 10:13).

God also promises that even if we are faithless, he will remain faithful, for he cannot disown himself (2 Timothy 2:13).That means in all circumstances, through all trials and hardships, he is there beside us, even when we don't perceive his presence. This is beautifully illustrated in *The Pilgrim's Progress.* In the episode where Christian, the hero, is invited to the house of the Interpreter, he is shown many symbolic pictures of the Christian life. In one room, he sees a fire burning next to a wall. Standing by the wall was an individual (representing Satan) continually pouring water on the fire to put it out, yet the fire burned higher and hotter. Christian is shown the other side of the wall, where another Person is continually and secretly pouring oil on the fire. The Interpreter explains, 'This is Christ, who continually maintains the work already begun in the heart by applying the Oil of His Grace. Because of this, the souls of His people remain full of grace in spite of what the Devil can do.' (quoted from *The Pilgrim's Progress in Modern English,* L. Edward Hazelbaker, ed., published 1998 by Bridge-Logos, Gainesville, FL). He will never fail us, forsake us or leave us, all because he is a faithful God who can never be unfaithful. He also promises that his grace is sufficient and that no matter how difficult life is, he is always there pouring the oil of grace upon the fire of our faith.

One of God's most wonderful promises is that he works 'all things work together for good to those who love God, to those who are the called according to His purpose' (Romans 8:28). If we belong to him through faith in Christ, everything that happens in our lives is in his sovereign control. He is behind the scenes managing, directing and supervising everything, and he either causes or allows all things according to his holy and perfect will and purpose. If that were not so, if there were something or someone else controlling things, then God would not be God. For those who love him and are his called ones, not only is he working all things together, but he does it in such a way to ultimately be for our good. Of course Mary understood this, either consciously or unconsciously, long before the verse in Romans was ever penned by Paul. This terrible fate that awaited Jesus would be one of those things that God would work together, not only for her good, but for the good of the human race. Only that kind of faith could enable her to rejoice in what was about to unfold, to anoint Jesus for his burial, and to worship him freely and confidently.

God's most precious promise is the forgiveness of sin, victory over death, and eternal life for all who believe. Mary understood that, as much as she loved Jesus and wanted him to be with her, it was much more important for him to go to the cross. She saw first-hand his power over death when he raised her brother from the grave, and she knew that he would use that same power to save her from sin and raise her to eternal life where she would be in his presence forever. Seeing the big picture, as she did, will help us to fix our eyes on the promise of the glories of heaven. When we have that eternal perspective, the things of this life seem dreary and dull by comparison.

## A Mary Faith

Having a Mary faith in the modern world also means that we are to expect opposition. There are so many reminders of that fact in Scripture, but it is still a hard truth. No one wants to be opposed, ridiculed, or belittled for their faith. No one wants to lose friendships or upset family harmony. But Jesus said this is exactly what we should expect and be prepared for. He said he came to bring a sword which would divide us from our family members and cause division (Matthew 10:34–36). His two-edged sword is the truth of his Word. It always divides and those schisms can be very painful.

Because we are not of this world, we are to expect to be hated by the world for Jesus' sake, as he plainly stated in John 15:19:

*'If you were of the world, the world would love its own. Yet because you are not of the world, but I chose you out of the world, therefore the world hates you.'*

We are thought to be fools by those who reject Christ, and the world does not treat kindly those who are perceived as foolish. But this, too, should be expected. It's not easy to be viewed by others, especially family and friends, as silly, irrational or idiotic. But it is inevitable. Paul encouraged the Corinthian church with these words:

*For the message of the cross is foolishness to those who are perishing, but to us who are being saved it is the power of God* (1 Corinthians 1:18).

In the face of opposition, we must defend the truth, not ourselves. Understanding that faith is tested daily to reveal its reality to us goes a long way to helping us endure the opposition. Just as gold is refined by fire to remove the impurities, so our faith is refined by the conflicts it naturally produces in a world that has rejected our Lord:

*In this you greatly rejoice, though now for a little while, if need be, you have been grieved by various trials, that the genuineness of your faith, being much more precious than gold that perishes, though it is tested by fire, may be found to praise, honor, and glory at the revelation of Jesus Christ* (1 Peter 1:6–7).

Mary understood firsthand the reality of opposition, and she faced it with grace and submission to the will of the One who purposes all things according to his perfect will.

Having a Mary faith also means coming to the unshakeable conclusion that faith is resting, not doing. Like Noah's dove who could find no rest for her feet and her weary wings until she returned to the ark, so we must constantly return to Jesus and find rest in him. The picture of the exhausted dove returning to Noah is a beautiful foreshadowing of Jesus' work on our behalf: 'So he put out his hand and took her, and drew her into the ark to himself' (Genesis 8:9). We come to Jesus for salvation, and he draws us to himself where we find rest and eternal life in him. But we find the same rest again and again as we venture out onto the stormy waters of life only to find no place for our weary feet. Then Jesus puts out his hand and draws us back to himself where we find rest for our souls. Again and again throughout our lifetime on this earth, he says, 'Come to Me, all you who labor and are heavy laden, and I will give you rest' (Matthew 11:28).

Faith is resting in the nail-scarred hands of Jesus, confident in his finished work on the cross for us. His work was fulfilling the laws of God, *all of them*, so that there is nothing left for us to do to gain his love or maintain it. When he said on the cross, 'It is finished', that's exactly what he meant. No longer are we burdened by the requirements of the law, not even those requirements we put upon ourselves or those put upon us by others. Time and time again as we weary ourselves with the do's and don'ts of the Christian life, he is waiting for us to come back to him for rest. That kind of faith, the Mary kind, is the unwavering confidence that we can rest in God who will never fail to sustain us, especially in times of trial or persecution or sorrow. Mary's faith stood the test of each one of those things, and she came out of them with a faith that was her crowning glory and a memorial to her forever.

No doubt someone reading this is thinking *what do I have to do to have a Mary faith?* Our natural inclination is to seek out another to-do list. But you will find no encouragements here to attend church more often, get into more Bible studies, give more money, or do more at church. The only way to have a Mary faith is to dedicate ourselves to truly knowing God, first by praying for the desire to seek him continually and the wisdom to discern the truth about him from the falsehoods. How vital it is for us to think clearly about God! To know him and his attributes. He is a righteous God who will not allow an injustice to continue forever. He is a faithful God who always keeps his promise. He is a merciful God whose compassions fail not. He is an omnipotent God and nothing is too hard for him. Through his sovereign control, he is able to overrule even the wicked actions of men for the good of his children and the glory of his name. Indeed, having a Mary faith starts and ends here—knowing God intimately and resting in him.

# Epilogue

When I decided to undertake the project that became *Memorial,* I knew I was embarking on a writing endeavor unlike anything I had previously done. In tackling the mystery of Mary of Bethany, I was venturing into potentially controversial waters. It's relatively easy to write about the apostle Paul or Peter because so much is revealed about them in the Bible, what they did, what they said, even their emotions. But Mary, being the silent, enigmatic creature she is, presented a unique challenge. Unraveling her mystery required a good deal of reading between the lines and putting seemingly unrelated passages together to come to conclusions that are not at first obvious. But that's the beauty of the Word of God. Reading through the Bible in a year may be a worthwhile goal, but if you take the time to dig deeply into just a few verses, riches beyond your imagination can be yours. That is what I found in my study of Mary.

As I was digging into each verse, uncovering nuggets

of wisdom about Mary, I was reminded of a story I once read about the extremely rich, upper crust socialites of the early 20th century. Known for their extravagant parties, one creative host treated his dinner guests to a unique table favor. A long cedar box ran the length of the table, just in front of the place settings. In the box was beach sand, along with small diamond-encrusted shovels, one for each guest. Then the host invited the guests to dig into the sand for their 'party favors'— diamonds, rubies, emeralds and sapphires. Excavating the gems of Scripture is very much like that. And it only stands to reason that the Bible, which contains the knowledge of an infinite God, would itself be infinite. We can only scratch the surface of it in a lifetime of study, yet another evidence of its divine authorship.

But the process of seeking to discover the real Mary was not without its potential pitfalls. In the course of studying and writing, I was aware of feeling a certain amount of trepidation. The last thing I wanted to do is come to wrong conclusions about Mary, lead my readers astray, or write anything that was unbiblical or misleading. And that is where I came to understand that without the continual intervention of the Spirit on my behalf, I might be treading on dangerous ground. My daily prayer became, 'Lord, please give me wisdom and discernment and please don't let me write anything that is not from you.' When I came to certain passages, such as the incident where Martha meets Jesus on the road, again I sought wisdom from God as to how to interpret it and how it fit in with the narrative of Mary. The significance of Martha's entire story struck me like a thunderbolt one evening and took me in a direction I had not anticipated. That opened up more truth about the necessity of knowing the Person of Jesus Christ, aside from what he did then or does today. I have no doubt that was from God because I would not have come up with it on my own.

Another thing I learned is, while commentaries have a certain amount of value, nothing is as important as reading the passages and letting the Bible interpret the Bible. I gained insight into difficult passages by looking at the Greek words, but ultimately the truths of Scripture are revealed by the Spirit through the literal reading of the texts. Jesus promised that the Spirit would lead us into all truth, teach us all things, and remind us of everything Jesus said (John 14:26). This is no more valid for pastors, teachers or writers than it is for every Christian, and it is equally true for men *and* women. I want so much to encourage women to know that we don't have to be professional theologians to understand the 'deep things of God.' The same Spirit that dwells in all Christians reveals them to us (1 Corinthians 2:10). But truth is rarely found in tweets. The knowledge of God cannot be reduced to 140 characters. Building a Mary faith through tweets and snippets is like trying to gain weight eating nothing but a leaf of lettuce each day. No wonder we are spiritually starved.

We have seen that the solution to the mystery of Mary is her extraordinary faith. But that solution brings up another mystery, one that won't be solved to the satisfaction of the finite mind of man. Jesus praised Mary for her astonishing faith, but that faith, as Ephesians 2 tells us, is a gift from him. So is it Mary who deserves the praise? Or is it Jesus, the author and perfecter of her faith? Or is it both? Like so many of the imponderables of Scripture, we won't solve that mystery until we are in heaven, if then.

I look forward to meeting Mary in heaven one day. I pray that all who read this book will be there with us.